Tes

from Hilltc

"I went to Hilltop to have a special time to empty myself of all of the stuff that preoccupies me and allow the Spirit of God to fill me anew. I did and He did."

Dr. Barry Corey

President, Biola University

"We just wanted to express our sincere gratitude by thanking you for such a wonderful retreat. Many have traveled extensively internationally (especially with previous corporate careers) and all were blown away by the retreat center/ mountains, the food, and the Christ-centered hospitality of your group. More importantly, during our recap sessions, the group expressed breakthroughs in relationships, finding rest in God, and a strong encouragement in their sense of calling and journey with God."

William J. Quay

World Vision

"It is such a blessing to spend time at our Lord's beautiful Hilltop, speaking the truth in love while growing in Him together as sisters in Christ."

Patty Liu

Biola Ruby Women Leadership Team

"The heart never forgets especially when the heart has been given space and time to be with God. My time at the House of Solitude was so rich. Not easy or light, but rich and significant for my soul."

Susan Johnson, MA

Adjunct Faculty, Talbot School of Theology/Biola University

"We were much in need of rest and retreat following my brother's passing and then my uncle's funeral. It makes such a difference in our lives to practice retreat."

Dr. June Hetzel

Dean, School of Education, Biola University

"Our lives have been extremely hectic and busy these past six months and our time at Hilltop has allowed us to refocus on God and our marriage in peace and solitude. We really enjoyed reading the books from the library, eating lunch on the deck, hiking the trails, and sitting on the bench at Inspiration Point."

Andrew Yap, DDS and Shirley Yap

"What a blessing our retreat at Hilltop was! We were so comfortable here and we gratefully appreciate every detail that has been thought out; i.e., the rocks along the hiking paths, the decked-out kitchen, and the inspiring prayer room."

InnerCHANGE, L.A., NOVO

Hilltop

How a Vision, a Wildfire, and a Series of Miracles Led to a Place of Rest for God's People

Gene & Judy TenElshof

Copyright © 2022 Gene and Judy TenElshof

All rights reserved. No part of this book may be reproduced or used in any manner without the prior written permission of the copyright owner, except for the use of brief quotations in a book review.

To request permissions, contact the publisher at Gene@HilltopRenewal.org.

Paperback: ISBN 978-0-578-36497-1

Ebook: ISBN 978-0-578-36498-8

Library of Congress Control Number: 2022901868

First paperback edition February 2022.

Edited by Drew Tilton

Cover and layout design by Natalie Lauren Design

Cover photo by Silas Cole

All Scripture quotations, unless otherwise indicated, are taken from the Holy Bible, New International Version®, NIV®. Copyright ©1973, 1978, 1984, 2011 by Biblica, Inc.™ Used by permission of Zondervan. All rights reserved worldwide. www.zondervan.com. The "NIV" and "New International Version" are trademarks registered in the United States Patent and Trademark Office by Biblica, Inc.™

Scripture quotations marked (TLB) are taken from The Living Bible copyright © 1971. Used by permission of Tyndale House Publishers, a Division of Tyndale House Ministries, Carol Stream, Illinois 60188. All rights reserved.

Published by Gene and Judy TenElshof

HILLTOP RENEWAL CENTER

HilltopRenewal.org

Dedicated to all who seek and find their home in God.

Table of Contents

PROLOGUE

FIRE!

Natural disasters never come on schedule. They don't care about human calendars and plans. Cataclysms like hurricanes and earthquakes come whether we are ready or not.

The San Bernardino wildfires were one such untimely disaster and, for Gene and Judy TenElshof, the fires didn't just come at the wrong *time*, they came while Gene and Judy were in the wrong *place*.

It was October of 2003 and Gene and Judy, long-time residents of Southern California, were thousands of miles away from home. They were in Boston at the North American Professors of Christian Education conference, where Judy was scheduled to present a paper.

It was a good time in the TenElshofs' life. They had hit their stride: Judy was a Christian pastoral counselor who also taught at a seminary, and Gene had recently stepped down from a successful, decades-long career in corporate America in order to dedicate himself full-time to running the retreat center that he and Judy had spent years creating.

That retreat center was called Hilltop Renewal Center, and it was not just the result of years of work, it was also the result of a vision from God.

God had given Judy the vision for the retreat center in 1996, and then, through a series of miraculous interventions, had helped Judy and Gene bring it to life.

Hilltop Renewal Center was situated in the midst of the bone-dry forests of the San Bernardino mountains. The long, hot summer had baked the trees and ground to a crisp, and now the warm and unstoppable Santa Ana winds were blowing off of the deserts, over the ridges, and down into the valleys that led to the Los Angeles basin.

All it took was a touch of flame to set the whole thing off.

For Judy and Gene, far away in Boston, the news seemed at first to come in trickles. A mention of a news report, overheard between conference sessions. Then a phone call from the church group that was currently up at the retreat center. Confirmation of evacuation orders. Now not just one news report, but many. Floods of them. Horrible video from helicopters circling the area. Smoke everywhere, obscuring the devastation beneath.

All of it while Gene and Judy were thousands of miles away, holed up in a hotel room, helpless to do anything about it. All they could do was watch…and pray…and wait. Surely, *surely* Hilltop Retreat Center—a place of refuge, a place of refreshment, a place that existed for no other reason than that

God had told them to establish it—*surely* Hilltop would come through the storm of wildfires unscathed.

Hilltop belonged to God; surely God would protect it.

And then, after returning home, the news was no longer just rumors and generic reports, but instead came as a phone call from a neighbor, a man who lived up in the mountains next to the ridge on which Hilltop stood.

"I'm sorry," he said over the crackling line, "Hilltop is gone."

Chapter One

A Vision in the Night

Judy

The story of Hilltop Renewal Center is a story about the power and love of God. God had a plan that He graciously brought us into, doing miracle after miracle to bring it to pass. In the process, He taught us how to pray and how to love. We are blessed to have been a part of this journey.

And it all started with a vision.

Gene

People who have visions are sometimes depicted as wild-eyed revolutionaries, or unworldly prophets yelling in the desert, or laid-back hippies mumbling about world peace.

But real-life visionaries don't look like that. Usually, they're just sane, competent, normal people going about their sane, competent, everyday work.

It's their very sanity and competency and work ethic that make them the perfect people to bring a vision to life. That was Judy.

Judy

And I'd say that was Gene!

Gene

But having and executing a vision isn't about the visionary—it's about God. It's not about us and the vision didn't come from us. We just followed the marching orders that God gave, the vision that He sent.

Following that vision changed our lives, and the lives of everyone who's been a part of the Hilltop story.

Judy

I had never had a vision before.

But there's always a first time for everything.

The week that changed our lives was a little out of the ordinary, but only a *very* little. It was a conference week and the year was 1996. While conferences can be a nice change in the routine academic schedule for professors like me, they still come around every year—they're a change in routine, but they're a *normal* change.

What happened at this conference, though, was far from normal. In fact, it was life-changing.

I had been invited to this particular week-long conference because of my overlapping expertise in the areas of counseling, theology, and pastoral training. I worked at Talbot School of Theology, a school within the larger body of Biola University, whose campus was situated in a quiet suburb just outside Los Angeles. Though much of the seminary was devoted to delivering the hours and hours of theological and Biblical knowledge our students needed in order to become informed, prepared pastors, the seminary also knew that pastoring took more than just head-knowledge. It took heart knowledge—and that was where I excelled.

Though my theological training and background were also strong, my life had been dedicated to helping Christian ministers thrive spiritually and psychologically in their callings. I had spent years of my life counseling pastors and Christian leaders, helping them to pick up the pieces after various emotional and relational struggles—affairs, addiction, or just plain burnout—and that experience had birthed in me a longing to prevent those struggles from ever occurring in the first place.

I wanted pastors trained to be whole—healthy in mind, body, and heart.

Happily, there were others who saw that need too. Our seminary had been working on just such a training program for our students, and my colleagues were happy to see me spend a week at this conference. They hoped I would come back full of ideas to strengthen the spiritual formation program I was currently developing for them. Meanwhile, most of the other conference attendees were Christian ministers, pastors, and denominational leaders. Church Resource Ministries (CRM, today known as

NOVA), who was putting on the conference, was happy to have me there because they knew I would help the attendees to go deeper into their hearts as they worked on learning more about themselves and about God's plan for their lives.

Gene

In other words, Judy was there to minister to the ministers.

Judy

Paul Rhodes was one of the leaders of CRM. He was a vice president of the organization, but at heart, he was a pastor of pastors. He was a man God had called to come alongside the broken-hearted and those who were feeling despair and hopelessness. He and I were old friends. We had worked together for years at Lakewood First Baptist Church, where I had directed a counseling center. When I arrived at the conference, he said, "I am so glad you came! Come and join my table."

There at the tables, the conference attendees were working on life maps. In this exercise, everyone at the table worked on laying out the narrative of their lives thus far, seeing how God had used the events, circumstances, and people from their past to form them.

Though I was paying attention to the experiences of the others at the table, mindful of my responsibility to help them really engage with the exercise, I didn't just watch the pastors work. I knew that in a group like this it was important for everyone to participate, and so I laid out my own life map too.

Memories surfaced as I worked. Many of them were focused around my husband, Gene. Gene and I had married very young—young enough that it felt like we hadn't just grown older together, we'd grown *up* together.

Gene was a tall, reserved man whose combination of unfailing courtesy, blunt honesty, and steady affection had won my heart. His calm demeanor hid a lurking sense of good humor, and he had the kind of wry laugh that always surprised a smile from those who heard it. I don't think I've ever met anyone who wasn't put at ease in his presence.

GENE

And I had fallen in love with Judy's sparkling blue eyes and fearless heart. Judy was a foot shorter than me, with blonde hair to her shoulders, and she had a warmth that drew people in. She knew how to listen and how to care, and I was drawn to her intelligence, her understanding, and her determined spirit. I'd known instantly that *this* was the woman I wanted to spend my life with—and it was the best decision I've ever made.

JUDY

As I worked on my life map at the conference, I remembered what my life was like when Gene and I were young, while we were still dating and before we'd gotten engaged. At the time, I had just graduated high school and was still living with my parents. Though my parents always took good care of me, there was a feeling in their household that love was conditional—you had to earn it. And if you didn't measure up? Well, there wasn't going to be any grace for those who couldn't toe the line.

One Sunday, Gene and I went to church and sat in what my parents thought was the wrong pew. After the service, they poured their anger out on me, yelling at me and berating me. It wasn't the first time I'd been subjected to this kind of treatment. I can't even count how many times I'd been the focus of explosive anger. It was just what my life was like. But I was older now, and I decided it was going to be the last time I'd just stand there and take it, so I walked out. I left my home.

And I had no idea where I was going to go.

Gene

Judy and I were both Christians—even though God still had a lot to teach us!— so I took Judy to my pastor and explained the situation. He was a wise man. He could see that we were just two young, hurting kids who needed a place of refuge, and so he suggested, "Why don't you go to Gene's brother and sister-in-law? Go to their house and stay there tonight."

Judy

So I did what the pastor suggested, and it ended up changing the course of my life.

Gene's brother is named Harley and his wife is named Marilyn, but everyone calls her "Mert." Harley and Mert welcomed me in with open arms. They took one look at this tearful, defiant girl that their brother brought to them and said, "Yes, we can take her in."

I ended up living with them for three months, before eventually going back home again for a short while before Gene and I married.

Later, at the 1996 conference, as I was sitting at the table with these pastors, listening to their life experiences and remembering mine, I saw that time with Gene's family as a turning point, because that was the first time that I really experienced unconditional love. Mert and Harley took me in and loved me, and God used that experience to shape me, and to open up my heart to His love.

Now, looking back not just at my teenage self, but at the professional woman I was by the time I was sitting at that conference table, I can see that God used Mert and Harley's love in my life in a new way. Actively remembering their welcome during the life map exercise was important. God used those memories to open my heart and prepare me for the journey He was going to put us on.

He was getting me ready for our next assignment.

Gene

It wasn't the assignment Judy thought she was there for. She thought she was there for Talbot and for CRM—to strengthen the pastoral training program for the seminary and to aid the pastors who were already at the conference.

But God's purposes and plans aren't always the same as ours.

We would learn that over and over in the years to come.

JUDY

I did get an inkling of God's plan before nightfall though. I didn't know exactly what was going on, but that experience of opening up my life story at the table that day was so moving, so profound, that I knew *something* was up. I could tell that the Spirit of God was going to be doing something in my heart—which was ironic, given that I thought I was there to help open up *other people's* hearts!

But as I laid my life out, I could tell it was a God-moment for me. I could feel the Spirit saying, *This has nothing to do with Talbot, this has nothing to do with CRM. This has to do with what I'm going to do in* your *life.*

That instinct was confirmed by the wonderful people at my table. After hearing my story, and hearing all my current obligations and responsibilities, one of them spoke up and said, "Judy, with all that you're doing, you should have a vision for the future. What are you going to be doing five years from now? Ten?"

It was a terrible question, but only because I had nothing to say in response. It wasn't that I hadn't thought about it—in fact, Gene and I had been praying about it for years. But I had to answer honestly.

"I don't know," I said. "I don't know."

It was a bleak moment. I felt tears pricking the corners of my eyes, wanting to fall. Then, those wonderful, wonderful people around the table actually gathered around me, laid their hands on me, and started praying for me.

As I sat there, feeling the warmth of their hands on my shoulders, and the even greater warmth of their supportive presence, I heard their words swirling around me in a chorus of petitions. They asked God to bless me, to guide me, to give me a discerning heart for my future in ministry.

And then they asked that God would give me a vision.

Their faith must have been great because, even though they could have had no way of knowing it, God was going to answer their prayers for me that very night.

Gene

It's funny to look back on that week because while Judy was having this life-changing experience, I was just going through life as normal. In fact, I wasn't even home that week! My working years had been spent building a name for myself in corporate America and that week, as with many other weeks, I was out on the road. Business was my life, and if my company wanted me somewhere, that is where I went. I'd do the deal, I'd get the clients, I'd make it happen.

I loved my work, and I was good at it. Also, my work supported our family, and that was important to me. I wanted that money, I wanted to be that provider for us.

I had no idea how far God was going to take me from the things that I thought brought me security—the things I thought made my life matter.

Judy

The conference wasn't on our university campus, but it was close by. In fact, it was close enough that I was able to attend the conference during the day and then go home and sleep in my own bed at night.

I was grateful for that, but—as I did every time he was traveling—when I went back to that big, empty house all by myself, I missed Gene. His presence was always a comfort to me, and I hated when he was gone.

I was used to it, though, and it had been a long day, so I went through my normal nightly routine and went to sleep as quickly as I could. After all, tomorrow was going to be another long day at the conference—and tomorrow before I even got back to the conference grounds, I was expected to stop by the seminary to attend the morning chapel service. I knew I needed a good night's sleep to face the next day's work.

So I went to bed, expecting eight solid hours of unmemorable sleep.

That's not what happened.

Gene

What happened was that God woke her up in the middle of the night. I know—she called me later to tell me all about it!

Judy

I was deeply asleep when I woke up with a sudden awareness that God was asking me to do something. It was about two o'clock in the morning. He gave me the name of a man:

Jim Hamel. Jim was a businessman I had met about ten years earlier—and told me that He wanted me to ask this man for money.

But I had no idea what I needed the money for.

I was confused. I knew it was God, and what He was saying was clear, but I wanted to know what the money was for. This didn't seem to be an answer to my deep desire to know what my future in ministry held for me. Asking someone I had not seen in a long while for money was not exactly a typical life plan!

When I thought about it that way, it seemed crazy.

But, weirdly, it also *didn't* seem crazy. I think that was because it was just so clear to me that it was God.

Back then, I didn't usually have direct conversations with God—in fact, on the night of the vision, I didn't even know enough to ask God any questions about it! Now, years later, I've learned not only how to listen to God, but how to talk to Him. But I was new at all that back then.

Still, I knew who was talking to me, and what He wanted me to do. He wanted me to go and ask this man for money.

I didn't know why, but I knew I was supposed to obey.

And...well...that was that! I went back to sleep.

I had no idea that the vision would continue the next night. In fact, when I woke up in the morning, I just went about the activities I had already planned: first to the seminary to attend chapel, and then back to the conference to continue helping the pastors and missionaries go deeper into their hearts to learn what God had for them.

At the seminary chapel, I sat down next to one of our philosophers. We got to chatting, and he asked how I was doing, and I couldn't help myself, I had to share what had happened the night before with *someone*, and so I found the words just falling out of my mouth.

"I think God's doing something in my life," I admitted, and I told him about my experience of being woken up the night before and about my orders to go and ask this man for money. "But," I concluded, "I have no idea what the money's for!"

He laughed. It was a deep, amused chuckle. "Oh, I don't know," he said, "I can think of *lots* of things the money could be for!"

I couldn't help it, I laughed too. But even as I laughed, I shook my head. "No," I said. Nice as it might be to have an influx of cash—and little as I knew about visions from God—I knew enough to know that get-rich-quick schemes were not exactly divinely inspired! "No," I said again, "I'm pretty sure that's *not* how it works!"

I drove from the university campus to the conference grounds, my head spinning. Though I was soon caught up in my role as a facilitator and learner there at the conference, my mind still kept going back to what God had told me. What did it mean? What was it for?

What was God's plan?

I went back home. I got ready for bed. I went to sleep.

And then God woke me up *again*.

This time, He told me what it was for. He told me it was for a renewal center.

I hadn't spent all day at a conference focused on prayer for nothing. *This* time, I asked Him questions.

Where? I asked.

Arrowhead.

Arrowhead? That was a small but popular vacation town up in the nearby San Bernardino mountains. Boating in the summer, skiing in the winter, but...Arrowhead?

Gene and I never went to Arrowhead. It wasn't a place I knew a lot about. Why would God send us there?

But our pastor had a house up there—in fact, I happened to know he was looking to sell a particular property he owned. Maybe that's what this was about? Maybe that's what the money was for?

So I asked God.

But He didn't answer, and so the answer was clearly *no*, and there I was, as puzzled as ever.

God didn't leave me in confusion though. For the rest of the week, the pattern continued. I kept going to the conference, and I kept waking up in the middle of the night, and hearing more from the Lord about what I was to do.

By the end of the week, my mission was clear: I was to found a renewal center for pastors, it was going to be near Arrowhead, it was supposed to operate debt-free.

And there was one last thing—a promise from God that warmed my heart—I wasn't going to have to do it alone. Other Christian organizations were going to share the vision and come alongside us and help us bring it into reality.

In the Lord's kindness, He took away my doubt. I found

myself at the end of the week with my marching orders, and what's even better, I *believed* in them. I knew this was what I was supposed to do.

But I was also faced with the seemingly impossible. If this was going to happen, it was going to take hundreds of thousands of dollars—and even more hundreds of thousands of hours of work. Who was God going to send to help bring this vision into reality? Who was going to work alongside me?

And, most pressing of all...what in the world was Gene going to think when I told him?

Chapter Two

Where We Were Coming From

Judy

To understand why receiving this vision was such an earth-shattering event for me, you have to understand where I'm coming from. I can only tell you—in what I have to classify as an understatement—that it was *not* my habit to receive visions from God! And it wasn't Gene's habit either.

Gene

Yes, as I like to say, we're not vision people. We are Dutch, we are Reformed, and we don't talk about visions.

Dutch Reformed people don't even *get* visions.

Judy

Our religious background really shaped us. I'm grateful for so much of what I learned from my church growing up—about

God and who He is and how we're to follow Him! But there was so much I hadn't learned yet. I hadn't really learned to pray. I hadn't really learned to listen to God, to hear Him.

I had come from a church that was very evangelical, but also very religious in how they approached their relationships with God. There were a lot of rules, a lot of *dos* and *don'ts.* There wasn't much freedom to interact with God on a personal level.

That conference week—the week of the vision—was amazing because God, in this short period of time, moved me from a place where I was helping others to see Him to a place where I could see Him myself. (And that helped me to help others more than I ever had before—I was able to help them in new and deeper ways!) I never would have guessed that He would want to do that kind of work in my heart. He gave me so much freedom in that week.

He taught me how to pray.

Gene

Judy says that week taught her how to pray, but I knew she had been praying for years at that point—especially for me. Five years before God gave her the vision, we'd gone together on a mission trip to the Philippines. It was the first time we'd really been able to minister together in any official sense and it was an amazing experience. It left us both interested in the idea of finding more ways we could minister together.

It also was a trip that happened at one of the lowest points of my life.

JUDY

That low point came in 1991—which started out looking like a good year for us! It was the year our daughter, Tami, was getting married—and with our son, Gregg, away at college, that meant that both of our children were going to be out of the house. For a parent, that feels like a big milestone, and we were really happy for our daughter, Tami, and her new husband, Jerry.

Life was good. The kids had left home, gone to college, and were on their way to establishing their careers and finding their partners for life. That meant Gene and I felt like our lives had opened up. Being parents made us so happy, but there's happiness in starting a new adventure, too, and life as empty-nesters felt like a new adventure. New freedoms always make way for new dreams.

We were dreaming new dreams in the spring of 1991, and it felt good.

GENE

Yes, the spring of 1991 felt good.

But then, in the summer of 1991, I lost my job.

JUDY

That was a shock. Gene had worked at his company for twenty-five years—a quarter of a century! He was doing important work and he was good at it.

I'd say that back in those days, money was Gene's primary motivation. But is there any wonder about that? His corporate ambitions drove him because he was so well-rewarded in that world! And people usually tend to be motivated by the things that reward them. Gene's worth was recognized in the corporate world and so that world became his heartbeat. It mattered to him that he could go after Manager of the Year, and get it. And that he could go after the VP role, and get it.

His company had been such a blessing to us that we sometimes called them our "second mother." They provided well, we had friendships there, and we were often able to travel under their provision. When Gene had a business trip to go on, they'd often send a car to the house to pick him up and take him to the airport, where he'd fly out of the city—usually schmoozing his way into first class.

Gene served them for many, many years, and in a real way, I think that was training for the kind of service God would eventually demand of him at Hilltop. He knew how to serve; it was just that his servant's heart was directed to the wrong master.

But at that point, we couldn't see that. He worked for a great company, and they supplied all our needs. We never even *thought* of imagining life without them.

Gene

But in 1991, they were bought out by a larger organization, a company that immediately began downsizing. After the new company squeezed my colleagues and me for all the institutional knowledge we had, they began letting people go—and I knew that it was only a matter of time before I would be let go as well. I was told to report to the home office in Indiana, where I was met by Human Services, and offered a severance package. That was it. The meeting lasted fifteen minutes. By the time the quarter hour chimed, my office, my secretary, my position, and our income were all gone.

I was dazed as I walked out of the office that had been my home for years, and I was scared. Blinking in the sun, I found myself asking, "Who am I? What do I do with my life now?"

And even more importantly, "Well, what is it that I even *want* to do with my life now?"

Judy

After his layoff, Gene was asking big questions about his life direction—where he'd go in the next few years, who he'd be. But he didn't have time to ask *small* questions about his life direction—where'd he'd go in the next few weeks—because that was already settled: we were going to the Philippines!

Gene

That week, while sitting in our Sunday school class at EV Free, an executive pastor came in and asked for volunteers for Jim Adkin's singles group's mission trip to work on a building project in the Philippines. He was looking for a married couple to come along and help with the leading of this trip. I looked at Judy and said, "Well I don't have a job, so I am free to go, and you don't have school because of summer break."

We signed up to go on our first mission trip together—and it changed our lives forever. Judy ministered to the emotional needs of missionaries and I helped with the building project with the singles group. What an amazing learning experience it turned out to be! The culture, the weather, the food and how it was prepared, the experience of getting sick in a foreign country, and living with a shortage of water because of the flooding from a typhoon that hit while we were there—it was all incredibly memorable.

JUDY

Ministering to the ministers wasn't a new thing for me. It was already a part of my life as a counselor and as a seminary professor.

I myself was a seminary graduate and I'd been mentored by a man, Dr. Rex Johnson, who'd begun a ministry of training lay counselors and developing Christian counseling centers. I'd continued in this ministry after seminary, and eventually we'd established counseling centers in four different churches and in a Christian high school. Many of the Talbot students I worked with at Biola would come and do their internships in these centers that Dr. Johnson and I supervised.

My own practice consisted primarily of pastors and other Christian leaders. During those years after graduation, God had been growing my heart for the broken relational lives of these pastors.

Then, in 1989, I was asked by Talbot to do two things: to start working at their seminary full-time, and to go back to school for my own PhD, so I'd be better equipped for the work I was already doing for them.

I told the dean of Talbot that I'd agree to these two things—but only if I were allowed to create a program for Talbot that their students would be required to go through before graduation, a program that would reach their hearts and help to prevent the problems I was seeing in my pastoral counseling practice.

So, even back then, I had this awareness of the spiritual and psychological pitfalls that pastors face, and I had a growing desire to help as many ministers as I could to avoid those pitfalls. That was why I said yes to going on the Philippines trip to counsel the permanent missionaries on site there.

But I had no idea that when God led me into my PhD program and into full-time seminary work that I was being prepared for what He *really* had in store for me: the work He'd reveal to me in that 1996 vision.

GENE

Judy's work led us to the Philippines. And, even though I'd just lost my job, all of my old habits were still a part of me—including my work-honed habit of making friendly conversation with whomever I happened to meet in the course of my travels. So, on our flight across the Pacific, I struck up a casual conversation with one of the flight attendants. It was all going swimmingly until she asked the completely ordinary question, "What do you do?"

What did I do? I was stuck. What *did* I do? Horribly, I realized my first instinct was to answer, "Nothing."

But, as would happen time and time again on our faith journey, God provided a rescuer in the form of one of His people. The pastor sitting next to me leaned across and answered the flight attendant, cheerfully saying, "He's a missionary!"

Judy

It was a God moment, and one in which Gene's identity was clarified and confirmed: Gene was someone who was set apart to serve God, and to bring the message of God's love to other people.

Gene

In that moment before the pastor answered, I was stuck in a fog of doubt. But his answer was the sunlight that pierced the haze. *I* didn't know who I was, but God knew, and God made it clear.

It was a moment I never forgot.

Judy

The rest of the trip proved that pastor's quick, on-the-spot answer true; Gene was in his element serving others for the Lord's sake so that the gospel could be spread.

Gene shone in the Philippines. He enjoyed making new friends and was so good with all the people on site that the team soon gave him a new nickname: "The Mayor of Manila." I was busy with my counseling commitments, but Gene was there at the church construction site, pitching in with whatever needed doing.

He even wanted to pitch in with the cooking. The local folks would make dinner by just chopping up a chicken and throwing it into the soup. Gene hated that! He kept saying, "I can get into that kitchen and show them how to debone a chicken so quickly!"

I remembered that moment, years later, after Hilltop Renewal Center became a reality. At Hilltop, Gene was always the one who pitched in with all the practical things: painting, plumbing—and even cooking for the retreats!

Gene

Our time in the Philippines was a revelation. I was still focused on getting a job as soon as we got back to the States. I was still focused on going back to work. But there was something about being on the mission field with Judy—something about working side-by-side for the Lord—that was really good. Even with my career-focused mindset back then, I could see there was something for us in that kind of partnership.

Judy

I could see it too. We were really ministering. We were doing the same things in the Philippines that we did in our normal jobs back home—or at least, some of the same things. Gene was using his people skills and I was using my counseling skills. But we were using them in this focused, cooperative, God-centered way.

All of a sudden, all I wanted was *more* of that. I wanted to serve God, and I wanted to serve Him *with* Gene.

I had no idea how that could become a part of our everyday lives. At the time, it was just an aberration during a few weeks in a foreign country. I didn't see how ministering together could become the reality of our everyday lives.

But I'd spend the next five years praying that God would show me how.

Gene

I should point out: Judy kept praying about that.

I did not.

Judy

But that's part of the story! We grew at different paces, and in different ways, but we both grew. We both changed.

Maybe when it came to the desire to minister together, Gene grew more slowly than I did. But that's only fair, because in so many ways, I'd spent our marriage playing catch-up with *him.*

We married very young. He was twenty, and I was only nineteen. In a real sense, we grew up together—and in an even deeper sense, Gene had to parent me. We were only two years apart in our actual ages, but in terms of emotional maturity, I was much younger than Gene.

Gene's servant heart has always been a part of him. He served his colleagues in the corporate world for years, and he serves God with great devotion now, but from the time we fell in love, he's always been a servant to me, he's always taken care of me.

I had such an empty heart when we first got married. But Gene's filled it with the way he's loved me. I find his love so amazingly beautiful.

I'm not the only person who feels safe around him either. Our home has proven a safe refuge for many people over the years, and I think it's because of how Gene makes people feel at ease. You never wonder where you are with Gene—you never wonder if there's something he's hiding, or if he's being secretly judgmental, or if there's something he's not telling you. People aren't scared around him, because *he* isn't scared. He's not afraid to say what he thinks, and he's just not afraid *period*. He's comfortable in his own skin, and honestly, being around someone like that is incredibly healing—especially if you grew up in a rigid, rules-oriented household like I did.

I have a lot of filters, but Gene doesn't. He just is who he is, and people find that comforting. If he says you're welcome in his home, then you really are welcome.

GENE

That's true—I have few filters!

But to be more serious, I think what Judy's saying is right: our home has been a refuge for various people over the years. Maybe it started when our kids were teenagers, and we were constantly welcoming their friends into our home. Our house was the place to be! Our kids' friends felt comfortable there.

We've also had a few people live in our house for a couple of years, here and there. We've opened our doors to people who needed a safe space to heal—much like my brother and his wife did for Judy back in the day. We've tried to pay that forward. We've opened our doors to Judy's students, hosting things like graduation events.

Hospitality's been a part of our marriage for a long time.

Judy

Hospitality is also, as it happens, at the heart of what Hilltop Renewal Center is about! Hilltop is a place for people to come, to be welcomed, and to find themselves at home with God. It's a place of peace and beauty where all their physical needs are cared for so that their spirits are free to commune with God.

Coming home from the Philippines, we had no idea that our prayers about how to minister together wouldn't be answered for another five years—and no idea they'd be answered by God giving us the vision to build a retreat center!

But I knew, when we got back, that I wanted to keep doing Kingdom work with Gene. That trip really showed me that our marriage was made for that—that *we* were made for that.

Gene

I'll be honest, even on our return from the Philippines, I still thought I was made for work in the corporate world. I did see what Judy saw: I saw that we worked well together, and I knew serving God was important.

But back in those days, I had what I liked to call a personal relationship with the church—not a personal relationship with God.

I had a lot of head knowledge about the Bible, and I knew my doctrine, but to say that I actually lived out my Christianity day-to-day in corporate life just wouldn't be true.

I was more involved in climbing the ladder of success than thinking about how to serve the Lord. I wanted to get to the top of that ladder. My colleagues and I saw corporate life as *life itself.*

The thing is: once I got to the top, I saw that it was pretty empty up there. There was just *nothing* there.

But my whole identity was still wrapped up in what I did, rather than who I was in Christ. When I lost my job, I felt like a homeless person. I felt lost—and it was because all my identity had been wrapped up in my work. Without it, it was like I had no identity at all.

Judy

Looking at where we were at that point in our lives, starting a retreat center should have been an overwhelmingly impossible proposition. And considering where we were five years after we returned from the Philippines, the idea seemed even more far-fetched. Gene had long secured another corporate position and I was more busy at the seminary than ever!

I mean, look at who we were at the time that God gave me the vision. We were not independently wealthy billionaires who could just write a check for a new charitable cause. We weren't young people with no responsibilities who could just fling themselves, willy-nilly, into some huge new project.

We were people who already had commitments to work and family—commitments we intended to honor. There didn't seem to be room in our lives for starting a time-consuming, money-gobbling ministry from the ground up.

GENE

But if you look at it from another direction, we were *exactly* the right people for a job like this—and that was also because of who we were. We were a couple with a long history of serving together and growing together. We worked well together and we'd practiced hospitality together regularly over the course of our whole marriage.

And even my corporate experience came into it: I knew how organizations worked. I knew how money worked. I knew how to get a project started, keep a project going, and see a project through to the end. And even my layoff experience had taught me something necessary! It taught me that, eventually, chasing dreams of money and power will leave you empty. Even though I chased—and got—another good corporate job soon after our return from the Philippines, I couldn't forget that emptiness I'd found after I'd been let go. I couldn't ignore what I'd learned through that experience.

JUDY

God knew what He was doing when He put us through the experiences we've gone through in our marriage. He knew what He was preparing us for, even if we ourselves didn't have an inkling of it.

But, really, even though we're the ones it happened to, the story of Hilltop Renewal Center is not our story. It's a story about God and His miraculous power, and about how He moved obstacle after obstacle out of the way in order to bring His plans to pass.

We came home from the Philippines with a new desire to serve God together. But it would be five long years before God would give me the vision that would show us how.

Chapter Three

Gathering Supporters… and Believers

Gene

When I look back on it now, I can see how God used the events of our lives to prepare us for the work He wanted us to do. He is like a master sculptor and He uses our trials and experiences to shape us into the people He wants us to be—as surely as a potter uses a wheel to spin his clay into the pots he wants to craft.

But even though I can see God's handiwork in our experiences as I look back on them, on the day that God actually called us into this new adventure, I didn't see the bigger picture. I didn't feel like I'd just been prepped to jump into a huge new change with Judy. I wasn't on the same page as her.

In fact, I wasn't even in the same city.

Judy

During the week of the conference—the week when I received the vision—Gene was traveling for his corporate job, the new one he'd acquired after his old company was bought out. So, even though the conference was close enough to our home that I could return there to sleep every night, I wasn't coming home to my husband.

But I didn't let a little thing like distance stop me from sharing the vision with him. Keeping our relationship alive and close during times of travel was an old, old dance to us. We knew all the steps.

So, I knew communication was important, and I knew I had to tell Gene what the Lord had told me—even though I was sure it was going to be a much stranger phone conversation than we usually had!

I also knew I'd be asking a lot of him. After all, I wasn't just asking him to believe me. In telling the story, what I'd really be asking was, *Will you support me?*

Because what God was asking me to do was something that was going to upend our lives. It was going to change everything.

It didn't just involve my life, my choices, my career.

It was going to change everything for Gene, too.

Gene

And I realized that almost as soon as I picked up the phone to listen to her. I mean: it was obvious. You couldn't do a project like she was proposing without it taking over your whole life—not when you were starting from ground zero, with no money, no supporters, no experience, no blueprint.

Yet, big and unexpected as it was, I was surprised at how much the idea appealed to me. I could see how a retreat center like this might use her gifts and my gifts in complementary ways.

Judy

Yes! I was so surprised, so delighted, when Gene began to get excited about the idea.

Gene

Hmm. Excited? Maybe.

Cautiously excited, I'd say. *Guardedly* excited.

After all, I was still of the opinion that we were not vision people. We were Dutch Reformed people.

And, as I said before, Dutch Reformed people don't get visions.

Judy

That might be so, but what struck me that day wasn't any kind of unwillingness to believe on Gene's part. Rather, what made an impression on me was, again, how wise he was. How practical. He heard what I had to say, and instead of expressing doubt, he asked questions—and they were such good, helpful questions!

Gene said things like, "How will we be able to finance this? What will we do with our home?"

But I could tell, as we talked, that he was leaning in. He was getting engaged with the idea.

Gene

That's true: I was. Even then, at the very beginning, I could feel myself being drawn into the plan.

I think it was Judy's conviction and clear passion for the idea that really painted the picture for me: when she talked about it, I could *see* us doing it. I got more and more involved in it as I listened to her.

Despite my prejudice against visions, I found myself thinking, *This could be real.*

Judy

But Gene was still cautious about it, and I honestly appreciated that. We're a good balance for each other there.

I remember him pointing out that there was still one more day to the conference, and he recommended that when I returned to it, on Sunday, I should consult with CRM, and see what they thought of the vision.

"And then," Gene promised, "when I come home on Sunday evening, we can *really* talk about it."

I agreed, and as I hung up the phone, I thought, *Maybe this is it—maybe, after all these years of praying, God is finally going to give us a way to serve Him not just on our individual paths, but to serve Him* together.

GENE

I knew that Judy consulting with CRM was going to be important. After all, I'd learned the importance of teamwork and buy-in during my time in the corporate world. And CRM were Judy's people—they were her peers. They were well-positioned to know whether or not this was a good idea.

JUDY

But the next person I ended up telling about the vision wasn't anyone from CRM. Instead, it was our son, Gregg.

GENE

And come to think of it, that was my fault, too!

JUDY

Yes, it was! Gregg called me because he had talked to Gene. He basically said, "Dad told me something significant is going on in your life, and I'd like to hear about it!"

So I said, "How about we go out to lunch—maybe Sunday noon, after church?" It would just be Gregg, his wife, Laurel, and me, since Gene was still out of town.

We went to a restaurant called Mimi's. It was decorated like a French cafe—the outside terrace was filled with bright flowers overflowing from large brick planters, the inside was filled with cute little tables, and the delicious smell of freshly baked bread wafted out of the kitchen, making our mouths water.

Gregg and Laurel and I followed the hostess in and took our seats. After the waitress brought our water and took our order, Gregg said, "Okay, tell me everything."

So I began sharing the story of the vision, and they listened attentively. When I got to the part about the retreat center being somewhere around Arrowhead, something inexplicable happened: Gregg and Laurel turned and looked at each other, their eyes filling with tears.

Then they turned to me and said something amazing. They said, "We know where."

I felt the Holy Spirit moving in my heart in that moment—and it turned out that Gregg and Laurel felt the same thing.

I said, "How can you know where?"

They explained to me that they had just come back from a trip to Lake Arrowhead! They'd stayed with friends at a home owned by the father of Laurel's college roommate. They'd gone up there with the sole purpose of having a relaxing weekend—the plan was just to have some fun in the sun out on the lake. But, instead of splashing and swimming, they found themselves spending some significant time in worship—both together and separately. It seemed to be something about the wonderful house where they were staying.

The property was set up in such a way that there were small areas where individuals could get away and find solitude, but it also had porches that were perfect places for building community. In fact, they'd started remarking to each other, "This house would make a great place for a retreat!"

The whole group of friends who were up there on vacation together found themselves naturally seeking time alone with God, and time together in worship—without any scheduled program prompting them to do so! It had been a wonderful time of renewal, and they were eager to share about it with me.

There was one other weird thing. Gregg and Laurel said that while they were still up in that house in Arrowhead, they had both, individually, pictured Gene and I in that setting. "We saw you up there with people, and Dad was cooking, and it gave us this sense that you were going to be up there somehow, and we didn't know what it meant. But now we know."

Gregg added, "You know, if this comes to pass, it will be the greatest miracle of our lives."

Laurel agreed, and then added, "And here's one more weird thing: that wonderful property? It's for sale!"

Gene

When I heard about that part later, it stuck with me. What a coincidence, right? That's the easy reaction to something like that.

But the further we got in our journey, the easier it was to see that *coincidence* is the wrong word for something like that.

A better word is *providence.*

Judy

Yes! Along with their enthusiasm about Arrowhead, Gregg and Laurel were also enthusiastic about the idea of the renewal center itself. As I shared about it with them, they were able to picture it easily. It almost seemed like it was a reality already—and that mattered to me, because they were our kids, and they knew us really well. They knew our gifting. The fact that they could easily picture Gene and I putting together an effective and nurturing ministry for the renewal of Christian leaders meant a lot.

But then came the moment they shared about the house they'd stayed in up at Arrowhead! It was such a Holy Spirit moment—and we felt it, all three of us.

It was exciting and it was scary. Right afterward, Gregg said, "If this comes to pass, we will never forget this lunch."

And we have never forgotten that lunch.

GENE

That was the beginning of Judy's quest to seek out the supporters that God had promised. But it was hardly the end.

JUDY

Not even close! For one thing, I still had to follow Gene's advice: I had to go and share the vision with my friends at CRM, back at the conference.

When God gave me the vision for a renewal center for pastors, I understood the need and I accepted the call. But I was still left with the question: would anyone else join me?

Now I knew that my family was on board—or at least was excited about the idea—but there was still God's promise that other Christian ministries would support this new dream. Would CRM be one of them?

I knew that it was my job to find out.

So, after the lunch with Gregg and Laurel, I went back to the conference.

I admit, I had a bit of trepidation, but this was the same group of pastors I'd done all that table-work with earlier in the week. We had already shared our life stories. We had gotten to know one another's hearts.

I couldn't be anything less than honest with a group like that.

And they repaid my honesty richly. They listened so attentively as I told them, truthfully, that it was their prayers for me that had opened my heart in preparation to receive this vision. Then I shared the vision itself with them, and their response was overwhelmingly generous—and enthusiastic!

In fact, one of them, my friend Paul Rhoads, encouraged me to share it with the CRM leaders.

I took his encouragement as my next set of marching orders and told CRM's CEO and VP about my vision.

Then something astonishing happened: they said that a retreat center was the project that was next-up on *their* to-do list. "We would love to join you in this," they said, and they invited Gene and me to come up to their headquarters in Yorba Linda the very next week.

Gene

It was truly astonishing. By the time I got home from my business trip, within the space of just a few days, Judy had been given a vision, told what she was going to do, what geographical area she was to focus on, that the center was to be debt-free, and that she would be joined by others—and that last promise was already coming true!

JUDY

When Gene got home, we talked about everything. But what I remember most was talking about the house that Gregg and Laurel had stayed in up in Arrowhead, because they had given me more information about it, and I was intrigued.

The house was called "Hilltop." That name was written in large letters over the garage. And what Gregg and Laurel had said was true: the house *was* for sale.

The only catch? The asking price was $3.2 million.

GENE

When she told me that number, I said, "God doesn't want us to spend $3.2 million on a renewal center." I've learned a lot about God's abundance and generosity in the years since, but back then, I pictured God as the sort of careful, conservative person who wasn't going to spend millions of dollars on a property to serve pastors.

JUDY

And I replied, "God owns all the money in the world. To Him, $3.2 million is only pennies."

But inside, I wondered how in the world the vision was going to come to pass.

Gene

From that point on, we prayed and searched the scriptures. We seemed to receive more and more affirmation. The location, too, seemed to be further confirmed when we traveled up the mountain to view the property with our longtime prayer partners. It became clear, without a doubt, that this was where God desired us to focus.

Judy

The more we prayed, and read, and waited, the more and more excited about it I got. I began to think, *This could be real.*

Gene

One of the things I did, after having a bit of time to let it all soak in, was to call my brother, Harley, and to tell him all about it.

Harley responded the way any decent brother would: with good-natured opposition! He grilled me on the financial issues, he stressed the improbability of the whole thing... "But," he added, "I can tell you've been really smitten with this!"

Judy

Other than my family and the folks at the conference, I was slower to share my vision with others. But I began to do it, a little at a time: a friend at Fuller here, and acquaintance who I knew had a heart for pastors there. Everyone seemed to resonate with the idea that pastors needed help, support, and training—not just eventually, but soon!

One friend sent me a message that was particularly meaningful to me. She sent me a card, inscribed with the words of Habakkuk 2:3-4:

> And the Lord said to me, write my answer on a billboard, large and clear, so that anyone can read it at a glance and rush to tell others. But these things I plan won't happen right away. Slowly, steadily, surely, the time approaches when the vision will be fulfilled. If it seems slow, do not despair, for these things will surely come to pass. Just be patient! They will not be overdue a single day! (TLB)

I returned many times to that passage from Habakkuk, pondering it prayerfully and wondering how God was going to bring the vision into reality. Those verses held me for a long time. They assured me that the vision was going to come to pass, and that was a significant support to me in those early days of waiting.

And there was a lot of waiting! After the overwhelming amount of confirmation that the week of the vision had brought, it felt as though everything would come to pass within the next week. Or at least the next month. Or at least the next year?

But God had a different plan for accomplishing His promise.

Still, whenever I felt overwhelmed—even if it was only because I was trying to accomplish steps toward the vision in my own strength—God was merciful to me. He never let my spirit wane for long. He continually confirmed the vision through circumstances, people, and scripture. He let me know I was to keep moving forward.

Gene

And the next step in moving forward was to have the promised meeting with CRM. I went with her to their offices, with the plan of working on the vision. We wanted to further clarify and define the need, and discuss what we all might be able to do together.

Sam Metcalf was the president of CRM at the time, and he was very welcoming to us. It was clear that a renewal center was something that they wanted to do—it wasn't a hard sell, at all.

Judy

No, it was clear that God had laid this need for support of pastors on their hearts as well, and when we came and presented this solution, it was a solution they'd already been actively seeking. They were excited to hear about it, and said, "We will be your first Christian organization that will join with you and make this happen."

Gene

It was so good to have their expert help; as a worldwide organization, they knew what they were doing when it came to communicating with potential donors! They also helped us to put together both a brochure and a PowerPoint presentation that described our new mission.

I knew that these would be vital tools as we started inviting people in as new supporters of the vision.

Judy

That day with CRM was another instance that proved that the vision wasn't *my* vision—it wasn't just about me, or even just about me and Gene.

It was about God: about His plan for His people.

And time and again, He would bring the right person to the right place at the right time to make sure His will was done.

There were so many people who were important in carrying out God's plan for Hilltop.

Gene

And we met a few more of those people just a short time later: Walt and Sherry Harrah.

Sherry was Gregg and Laurel's Sunday school teacher at Irvine Presbyterian Church, and they shared the vision with her and with her husband, Walt. After hearing the story, Walt felt that Sherry's dad, Ray Ortlund, would be interested in hearing about the vision. Ray was the founder of Pastoral Renewal Ministry (PRM).

Unfortunately, telling Ray about the vision in person had to wait a short while, because Ray was in the hospital at the time.

But after attending the morning church service at Irvine Presbyterian, Judy and I went out to coffee with Gregg and Laurel, and Walt and Sherry, and a few others.

Judy

It was another Holy-Spirit-inspired, defining moment—and it turned out to be the connection through which another wonderful organization would join the project.

As we sat together at a table, enjoying our coffee, the conversation was flowing beautifully. Nothing had been said yet about the vision. Gene and I, and Gregg and Laurel, were excited to share about it—but we held in our excitement, trusting that God was in control.

After a while, a stranger joined the table and was introduced to us as a lawyer who specialized in nonprofits. That prompted Sherry to look over to us and ask us to share the vision.

As we did, a synergistic passion seemed to flower from one person to another. Everyone at the table got caught up in the idea of the renewal center—it was the same enthusiasm that had met the idea every time we'd shared about it so far.

Gene

When Judy had finished sharing about the vision, the lawyer did something unexpected: he asked if he could pray for us.

Judy

We said yes, of course, and the lawyer began to pray. As he did, it seemed like every word coming out of his mouth was a word we'd felt coming out of our own hearts as we'd talked to God about the vision. It felt like a confirmation from the Spirit of God when the lawyer finished his prayer and said, with a firm conviction in his voice, "This is going to come about."

We never saw that lawyer again. He was like Philip in the book of Acts, coming upon the Ethiopian eunuch in the road—he was there, he ministered to us, and then he was gone!

It was like God sent that lawyer to pray our hearts out loud, to reassure us that God was with us, and then he left, his mission complete.

Gene

There was one more amazing *not-a-coincidence* that came out of that lunch with Sherry and Walt. Sherry *did* go ahead and share the vision with her father, Ray Ortlund, and learned that he already had a connection with the project. As it turned out, he was the longtime mentor of the man who owned the house up in Arrowhead!

Ray joined the team, representing his organization, Pastoral Renewal Ministry.

Judy

That was the pattern we continued to see from that point on: everything came about because God was going before us, preparing the way. He connected us with people we didn't know, people who could help us…but it was always *Him* doing the work, *Him* making the connections.

It wasn't us. It was God, bringing the body of Christ together to do something important that would have an impact on the Kingdom.

We didn't have money. We didn't have resources. We didn't have power. But we had a story—a vision that God had given us. And it turned out that was enough to move mountains.

Gene

Or at least to start a movement up *into* the mountains!

But what Judy says is right: it was all God, not us. That was clear from the beginning. But being allowed to work *with* God, to work *for* God...that was—and is—such an honor.

Judy

So now we had gathered a small group of enthusiastic people. It wasn't enough support for a full-fledged team, not yet.

But the project was beginning to gain ground.

Chapter Four

How Great the Need

Gene

As we talk about how the Lord was slowly helping us to build the team that would bring Hilltop Renewal Center into reality, it feels important to explain why any of this matters in the first place. After all, I can imagine someone asking, *Why would pastors need a renewal center? Aren't they at church all the time anyway? Aren't their lives one long, blissful session of prayer, worship, and Bible study?*

In short: no. No, they're not. Pastors' lives are complicated, busy, and full of stress.

And no one was more aware of this truth than Judy.

Judy

Yes—and the reason I was so mindful of the problems in pastors' lives is because I'd dedicated my career to Christian ministry and Christian ministers. Not only did I teach seminarians, I also had spent over a decade in Christian counseling—and the bulk of the people I saw in my counseling practice were pastors or long-suffering pastors' wives.

Pastors are often drawn to the ministry because they have a heart for spreading the gospel and for people who are hurting, but then, once they're actually *in* ministry, they find that helping people can become very overwhelming and they are not always sure how to help the people who come to them. Often their training has been focused far more on theology and the administrative work needed to lead a church.

Also, pastors themselves can be in pain relationally, mentally, or physically, creating multiple stressors. Consequently, pastors need help in understanding their own hearts. If they can be in a place of good spiritual and psychological health, they will be more able to lead their congregations into also becoming spiritually and psychologically healthy.

Affairs, abuse, addiction…those are just a few of the issues I've seen in my counseling practice. Sometimes those are issues in the pastors' own lives, and sometimes those are issues in their congregants' lives. But either way: those are issues pastors have to deal with.

Pastoring a congregation is not just a walk in the park.

Crisis after crisis revealed to me that pastors could easily forget their first love—the love of God that had drawn them into ministry in the first place—because they didn't know either God or themselves well enough. They didn't know how to care for their own souls, how to keep themselves daily in the Lord's presence in prayer, or how to attend to what the Lord was doing in their hearts.

Gene

I'd like to emphasize, again, that for Judy, these conclusions about the hard realities of pastoral life came out of hands-on, practical experience. If you can picture a surgeon, with his gloved hands bloody after re-stitching the guts of a trauma victim, you'd have the right metaphorical picture of what a counselor like Judy does. Counselors like her get their hands dirty in providing psychological first-aid to people who are emotionally bleeding out. She was really in the trenches with pastors, for years—and that was true even before she started teaching them in seminary.

Judy

Yes, much of my Christian counseling experience predated my life as a professor. I was asked by Dr. Rex Johnson to join him in his counseling ministry out of Lakewood First Baptist. Rex was a professor at Talbot. He loved the church and was a man with a strong call on his life—so many people became equipped to serve because of his work. I joined him in two of his ministries: *Innovations in Learning* and *Ministry Associates.* These ministries trained people in both seminaries and in local congregations in the work of counseling and of using their other gifts.

From our start at Lakewood Baptist, we worked on developing other counseling centers. I helped in the development, direction, and supervision of these ministries, and I also wrote manuals to guide our counselors in their work. Eventually we had counseling ministries established in four churches and a

Christian high school. Talbot seminary students would do internships at these centers, with Dr. Johnson and myself supervising them.

But back in the day, whenever we'd have pastors come to these centers, Dr. Johnson and I would take them on personally as our own clients.

I worked long hours there each week, spending my days both seeing clients and supervising, doing what God had asked me to be equipped to do. This work, although challenging, was incredibly rewarding. I was doing what I was made to do. I spent day after day both seeing clients and supervising Talbot students who were seeing their own clients. All of their stories rang in my ears continually. I was immersed in it.

On weekends, I'd sometimes give talks at local churches, and I'd have clients who came to me because of those talks. But it wasn't just the regular church members who'd come—it was often the pastors. That was very telling. It was like the pastors already knew they needed help; they just needed permission to seek it. Or they just needed to know *where* to seek it.

It didn't take long before my practice was pretty much all pastors—and their wives and families.

That leads me to note one of the other things I observed: many of these pastors' wives had similar issues and, eventually, enough of them came in for counseling that I started a therapy group made up solely of pastors' wives. They, as a group, were able to feel more heard and seen, and found support, as they saw others who were experiencing the same stressors and had some of the same kinds of anxiety and depression.

Often, if the wife did come in first, her husband would end up coming in later. Sometimes it would be because the wife needed him to be there because it was a marriage or family issue, but at other times, it was simply that the pastors became more comfortable receiving counseling because their wives were already there. Healing doesn't happen quickly. It's a process, and it took time for these dear women to take courage and ask for help when their husband was the pastor.

And the pastor would be in the dark about how to support his wife, about what it was she was struggling with—or even about his own role in her trauma. So as I began to work with these women and to help them speak up for their own needs, their husbands would end up coming in.

Other times, I'd see pastors run into trouble because of a sort of entrepreneurial blindness. They were so focused on numbers—on driving up church attendance—that they couldn't see anything else that was going on around them. They'd become business administrators, rather than shepherds of the flock.

I also had pastors get caught in emotional or sexual entanglements. That was always a heavy subject to deal with. And I was honored that they trusted me enough to work through these difficult issues with me.

And some of them were carrying burdens that were absolutely not of their own making. Many of them were wonderful people with wonderful visions of what they wanted to provide for their congregations, but they'd get so tangled up in the needs in front of them, that it was like they were a fish stuck in a net, unable to get free, unable to find God's good. They had lost sight of it.

There were just broken, broken pastors out there. My heart was weighed down with all the burdens they were carrying. I can still see their faces as I think about them today.

I'll give you an example. This happened in our university's old library—a library that has since been replaced by a larger, brighter, more open and modern building. But the old library was a sort of delightful warren of shelves and stairs and cubbyhole-like little annexes. You could have a conversation there and no one would hear you, because it was just such a maze of odd corners and turns and levels.

So I was there, in the midst of the stacks, and I ran into a pastor I knew, and we started to chat.

He was a bit frantic, clearly overwhelmed. I asked him what was wrong, and he said that he had five women from his congregation who'd been regularly seeking him out in his office—and all of them were abuse victims. "I can't move without one of them being there. They're calling me, they're babysitting for me, they've become such a part of our lives and I can't..." He trailed off. He cared deeply about these members of his congregation, he understood that they were hurting, and he wanted to help them. But he was being smothered by this huge pile of needs that he had no idea how to address. He wanted to help these women, but he didn't know how.

In the end, he sought out counseling, and so did these women from his congregation. Together, we were able to get help for all of them.

That was the kind of thing I was seeing. These pastors, who had such hearts for the hurting and lost, ended up (not surprisingly!) attracting lots of hurting and lost people. But once they attracted those people to the church, they didn't know what to do with them. They didn't know how to help.

Gene

What was different for Judy in those days was that she was working with mature pastors—she was working with folks who had been in the ministry for a good amount of time. And so, in those cases, counseling really was the answer. These pastors had established patterns that they needed to examine and deal with.

But I think the real game-changer came when Judy started teaching seminarians. That was when she saw a new strategy.

That's when it stopped being just about the cure.

It became about prevention.

Judy

Yes, when I came to Talbot, it was easy to see the opportunity. In fact, when I took the job, it was with the understanding that I'd be allowed to develop a program to help the seminarians with their personal spiritual development. Because I had seen firsthand how pastors' relational lives were often so broken, I now had a passion to reach their hearts *before* they went into ministry.

It's all a matter of spiritual formation.

Intentional spiritual formation is about having students understand the purpose for which they were created: to give God glory. God is given the most glory when we spend the necessary time with Him—allowing God to shape us more and more to reflect the image of God in which we were created. This comes through being with Him in all our activities of life. When we allow ourselves to reflect His image we are able to access every capacity we have and need in order to relate to God and others in a way that reflects who God truly is to the world. It isn't enough to know about God, we need to know ourselves, how God's design for us has been distorted by sin, and then we need to respond to the Holy Spirit's invitation to enter a process of transformation. This process most often includes not only spending time alone with God and practicing spiritual disciplines, but also spending time building authentic relationships with others in which our stories are shared and reflected on. In this we are able to see the movements of the Holy Spirit as He accomplishes His transforming work.

Spiritual formation makes people aware of their own hearts and of what God is doing, and helps them to focus on that, rather than on the clamor of the world around them.

These seminarians needed to learn to have an inward focus, at least some of the time, because the way to learn to see what God is doing is by becoming aware of your own heart and observing God's movement *there.* Every believer is indwelt by the Holy Spirit. That means He is always working in each believer's heart, because we are His workmanship (Eph. 2:10). By becoming aware of His work within, you are freed to look for His work in other people—especially people you're close to, like your spouse or your kids.

I wanted these pastors' ministries to flow out of the love that God gave them. I'd seen so many ministries that were reactive—where all of their work was in response to their people's needs—and I had a vision of their ministries instead becoming *proactive*, becoming purposefully directed out of the love that God had placed in their hearts.

That is something every pastor I met struggled with.

Gene

And, of course, Judy couldn't see every pastor in the world as a client! No one could. But she had a desire to meet these relational and spiritual development needs for as many pastors as she could.

Judy

Yes, and that's why teaching at Talbot felt like such an important opportunity! I thought, if we could train pastors, while they were still in seminary, to be more aware of their own inner lives and their own relationships, then when they entered ministry, they'd enter it with distinct advantages. I know lists can be boring, but I could see this long list of advantages unrolling like a scroll in front of me! With this training for pastors, they would grow more deeply intimate with God, learning to listen and respond to His voice, and to care for others as they felt cared for by Him. They'd be able to maintain their first love of God.

And that last one was so important, because love of God, and wanting to spread God's word, was what had brought them into ministry in the first place!

Gene

It's funny, because as Judy talks about this, I see it as a mirror to our own lives. The kind of awareness and attention that Judy wanted to cultivate in pastors-to-be was an awareness and attention that we had to learn how to practice in order to fulfill God's call to found Hilltop.

We had to learn how to hear from God ourselves. It's something Judy had been working on at the time of the vision, but I think it all came into focus for her during that conference week.

Judy

Yes! And we had to learn not just to hear from God, but how to listen to Him, wait on Him, respond to Him, and to find Him and His good in all things. I think that was where I experienced the biggest growth spurt. Moving from just *listening* into being able to have a *conversation* was an incredibly important start to this journey.

From a young age, I'd recognized God's voice when He spoke to me. I don't know how I learned to recognize it; I think it was just a gift from Him. For instance, I'd said that I'd never go to college. But God told me to go back to school and so I did. That was one of the first instances in my life when I had a clear knowledge that God was speaking to me, and that I needed to obey Him.

But moving into a conversational relationship with God came later. I learned to do that by learning to ask Him questions—in fact, I'd say that the way God taught me to ask questions was by giving me this vision that was so overwhelming and so all-encompassing that I *had* to ask questions about it. After all, I had so many!

GENE

I think Judy was also prepared to have that new kind of conversational relationship with God by the work she'd done around the conference table earlier in the week.

JUDY

Yes, the process of sitting around the table with those Christian ministers had a big influence on me. It helped me see how intentional you could be with God. Intentional in listening, intentional in asking questions.

It was as if, as I watched those pastors do the work of putting together their life maps—of deliberately opening up their own history and experiences in the presence of God and of one another—that I heard God saying, "This is how I work. I work through people. I work through your intentional questions. I work through your listening. I work through your prayer. I work through the prayer of others, and I work to make sure someone is with you in your brokenness."

GENE

And He works through the words of others. One of the people He worked through in Judy's case was Anne Graham Lotz, who had spoken in chapel at Biola the week before Judy went to the conference.

JUDY

Yes, her message really touched my heart. She said, "We need to be bold and courageous in regard to our callings." That resonated with me and I kept returning to it during the week and pondering it.

Looking back, I can see that God was using Anne's message to prepare my heart for the vision He was about to send.

He was preparing me to be courageous.

GENE

That's another important point: it was God who was doing the work. It's *always* God who is doing the work.

Sometimes spiritual formation is presented as a series of practices that will *make* you into the person God wants you to be. That's a bit backwards. It's not the practices that change your heart; the Spirit of God does that. Time alone with God, scripture memorization, fasting...all of that, by itself, won't change your heart.

JUDY

Yes. The message of spiritual formation often comes across as, "Do these practices and this good thing will happen."

What we really want to say is, "God is already doing this good thing in you, and these practices will help you hold your focus on what *God* is doing rather than what *you* want to do. Transformation happens and growth comes as we keep our hearts focused on Him."

The yeast is already in the dough. Putting the dough in a nice warm spot might be a good idea—but moving the dough doesn't mean that you created the yeast!

It's always God that gives the increase.

Gene

And God was the one we had to rely on in every step of this journey.

Judy

That was especially true as I faced telling my bosses what had happened to me the week of the conference. I'd received the vision, I'd shared it with my family and some close friends, I was convinced of the great need that it would address.

But I wasn't hired by the seminary to fundraise millions of dollars and then use them to found a renewal center! I was hired to teach, to counsel, and to do administration. And I was *committed* to that. I was committed to *them.* This vision seemed to direct me away from them, and that didn't just scare me: it broke my heart. I loved these people. And I owed them so much.

I didn't know how in the world I was going to tell them the truth.

Chapter Five

Admitting the Truth

Judy

After sharing the vision with Gene, our kids, the Harrahs—and even that nonprofit lawyer who'd shown up out of the blue!—it was hard not to feel like it was all-systems-go for launching the renewal center.

But the truth was that even though the vision had been confirmed by sign after sign (like our kids' connection to Hilltop and Ray's connection to its owner), there was still one big obstacle in the road, and it was an obstacle I could see no way over.

It was my current job.

Gene

That's right. At the time, Judy was teaching classes at Talbot School of Theology at Biola University, and the school was not only employing her, they were also financing her continuing education. They had an understanding that the

PhD and additional masters Judy was currently getting would be put to good use in the years to come—and not at some not-yet-existent renewal center, but right there, for them, at the brick-and-mortar school where Judy was already working.

Judy

The truth was that I felt beholden to Talbot, and not just financially! I had a moral obligation to them, and I also had an emotional attachment to them. These were colleagues and students I really cared about.

Plus, I loved my work! Before the vision came, I'd felt pretty sure that at the end of my PhD I was going to continue to teach full-time at Talbot and give them the rest of the years of my life.

Now I was afraid that the vision was going to pull me away from all that. After all, founding a renewal center was a gigantic undertaking—it wasn't something you could commit to halfway. I knew how the vision was going to include pastors, but not how it was going to include Talbot.

So how was I supposed to cut this Gordian knot? How could I be faithful to God's new call on my life, and also act with integrity toward my current employers? Employers who were, after all, also faithful followers of God!

The only thing I knew to do was to pray about it, and so that's what I did. "Lord," I said, "I can't see the way forward here. You have to resolve this one."

GENE

The answer didn't come right away. But in the meantime, we did continue to work on moving forward with the vision.

JUDY

Working with CRM to put together the PowerPoint and the brochure had been such a wonderful, confirming experience. But, if anything, having had that experience with them only made me feel more worried and self-conscious when I showed up at school, carrying this secret in my heart! I didn't know what my colleagues would say if they heard about the vision from someone else and, besides, I wanted them to hear about it from me.

I kept praying about it though. I knew I needed God to direct me in sharing the vision at the seminary. I wanted to do the right thing, at the right time, in the right way—and that took patience. I wasn't willing to be dishonest, but I wasn't going to make the mistake of being in a rush either. When you get worried and tense, and you let those negative emotions push you into hasty action, it's almost always a mistake.

Patience and prayer. Even when it's hard, patience and prayer are the way to go.

But, my goodness, the waiting was hard!

GENE

Yet God came through. We'd see that time and again in our journey: God provided.

His provision was never what we expected. But it was always what we needed.

Judy

Yes, God came through and—as would happen time and again—He came through in the form of one of His people.

This time, it was through one of my colleagues, a professor named Walt Russell. Walt was a professor of New Testament. He was also a dear friend and we were both a part of a Sunday night group that had been going strong for a decade. He loved God and the church, he mentored his students with love, and he taught the truth of God's word with the utmost integrity.

In May of 1996, about three months after the conference at which God had given me the vision, I was sitting in a faculty meeting at Talbot. Walt was running the meeting, and he was going through a long, committee-generated list of projects that the seminary wanted to put into action. You see, the seminary had an organization called Talbot Impact Ministry, or TIM, that was for big projects that the professors were involved in—projects they had dreams for, but that were big enough or different enough that they went beyond the day-to-day tasks of teaching our students.

So, Walt was sharing the long list from TIM when he got to one item in particular: a renewal center for pastors. He looked up from his list, looked straight across the table at me, pointed his finger, and said, "This one is still yours."

At first, I had no idea what he was talking about. I was too shocked. I hadn't told Walt about the vision—I hadn't told *anyone* at Talbot about the vision—and so how could he be sitting there at a conference table, pointing his finger at me, and directing me to go and do the thing that was uppermost on my heart and mind?

But then, suddenly, I remembered a conversation I'd had with Walt years ago: he'd told me that he thought I was the perfect person to develop a renewal center—not just for our seminarians, but for pastors and other Christian leaders.

When he'd presented the idea to me back in the day, I'd been overwhelmed—and not just with work responsibilities, but with my PhD studies at Fuller seminary, and with family and church responsibilities as well. So I'd said, "I'm so sorry, Walt. I know you think I should do this, but I just can't. I can't add one more thing to my plate."

It had been the sensible response at the time.

But here was Walt, years later, having *no* idea that God had given me this new vision for a center up in Arrowhead, bringing up this old request. He wanted me to know that the assignment was still waiting for me, if I wanted to take it up.

As soon as I heard him say that, it was clear to me that Talbot was meant to be involved with Hilltop.

And it was even clearer that God had gone ahead of us, once again.

Gene

Judy got home from that meeting and talked to me, and we decided together to call Walt and his wife, Marty, and set up a time to talk to them. Marty was an adjunct professor at

Talbot and had a big heart for the students there. She and Walt both had a gift of hospitality, which was shown in the way they had, over the years, invited many students in need to live with them for a time.

Judy

True to who they were, when we let them know we needed to talk, Walt and Marty invited us to their own beautiful home for the conversation. They asked for all the details of the vision, not wanting to miss anything of what God had done or was doing.

They then began to dream with us, planning next steps. Their excitement and faith helped us to believe and take courage.

Walt also asked us to join the TIM group for their next meeting and to share the vision there.

When I began at Talbot, I was the only female professor, and the TIM group seemed, to me, like an elite society. To have Walt invite me into it was so empowering, and it made me feel like I was being seen and known at Talbot for the first time. God was using Walt and Marty to show me who He had made me to be and who I could become. It was a sign to me that I really could do what He intended for me to do.

Truly, it was a privilege to share our story with people who I looked up to and respected so much.

It was also such a relief! Not just to have the vision out in the open, but to have it out in the open and welcomed with such enthusiasm by my colleagues!

It was also interesting, because every time we shared the vision, we got to hear a new reaction to it. All of the reactions were positive, but every person who heard it had a unique take on it—and I loved to hear and notice the small but important differences that arose from each new perspective.

When the Talbot professors spoke about the prospective renewal center, their focus was on it being a place where pastors could go to be alone with the One who made them, who could speak into their hearts about what He wanted them to do and be.

I treasured the professors' focus on how Hilltop would offer both solitude and the chance for ministers to hear a renewed call from God.

The other thing that happened when we went to the TIM group was that we were given another incredibly helpful connection: the TIM members encouraged us to talk to Biola's lawyer, Jerry Mackey. They explained that he had the knowledge and experience to help us create a nonprofit 501(c)(3)—a vital next step if we wanted to begin raising funds.

Gene

It was at this time that we formed our Board of Directors, which was made up both of Biola personnel and of folks from outside Biola. Judy was one of the Biola folks, and one of the others was the dean of Talbot, Dennis Dirks. Dennis was a man of such integrity that he was well-known and respected not only by the faculty at Talbot School of Theology, but also by all of the other schools that made up Biola University and beyond.

From outside Biola, we had me, and we also had Sam Metcalf, who was the founder and CEO of the worldwide mission organization CRM. We also had—wonder of wonders!—Ray Ortlund. Ray was a well-known and respected pastor, mentor, and author. He hosted a weekly radio program with his wife Ann, and it had an extensive audience. Ray was warm, decisive, and not afraid to take leadership and to share his beliefs and thoughts out of his wealth of experience.

Judy

Having Ray join our board was such a blessing and an encouragement! I had first learned of Ray by listening to his broadcast on the radio and reading his wife Ann's books. Later, we heard testimonies from young men who had been mentored by Ray and Ann, and of the fruit it brought to their lives.

After our son told us that Ray and Ann's daughter Sherry was their Adult Sunday School teacher, and shared about all they were receiving from her, I was so honored that she asked Gregg to bring us by one Sunday to share our vision with her.

Once Ray was home safe from the hospital, Sherry and Walt Harrah followed through on their promise to share the vision with him. So that coffee date with our children and Ray's children was what led to Ray joining our board—it really proved to be a divine appointment! To have Sherry take the vision to her father, Ray, who had founded Pastoral Renewal Ministries, could only have been a work of the Holy Spirit. We were so honored by Ray and Ann's interest.

Truthfully, everyone on the board was a blessing and an encouragement: Dennis' presence represented the approval and support of my employer and my colleagues, and Sam's presence showed the truth of God's promise to bring other Christian ministries into the effort alongside us. Having Gene there meant that this wasn't just my effort, but that it was ours together, as a married couple and as a family.

And Ray Ortlund's presence meant that the whole endeavor had the blessing and approval of someone I considered a senior statesman of Christian ministry.

Gene

Our first full, official meeting as a board was in a tiny room at Talbot—Feinberg 120, located in a semi-underground hallway down below the largest of the university's chapels.

At this meeting, Ray turned to me and Judy and said that several people before us had wanted to do a ministry like this, but that this was the first time he felt that the couple asking to do it actually had what it took to make the ministry a reality.

Judy

Yes, he said that we had the right connections with people—with Biola and with other organizations—and he also noted that Gene's business acumen would serve the new ministry well. Ray said, "These are the things that you guys have that will make the vision possible."

Gene

Our age was another point in our favor. We weren't young and inexperienced—weren't starry-eyed, naive dreamers—but neither were we too old to have a chance of seeing the plan all the way through to completion.

Our age wasn't anything we could take credit for, of course! But it was another factor that Ray saw as being an advantage.

So there in that little office, we had people and we had a vision, but we still needed a plan.

And that's what Ray gave us next.

Judy

Yes, Ray gave us our marching orders. He had such clarity of mind!

After we signed all the papers for the incorporation, Ray looked at me and said that there were three things that I needed to do—three next steps that would get us started on the practical aspects of making Hilltop a reality.

The first, he said, was that I had to finish my PhD. Ray said that he didn't want to see me become what they call "ABD" or "All But the Dissertation."

Gene

I should point out that Ray's fear there was grounded in reality. Not because Judy was particularly likely to opt out of finishing her degree—she's tough and persistent and I knew she was going to finish—but because *so many* doctoral candidates stumble at the end. I've seen numbers indicating that up to three-quarters of those who start their doctorate never finish. It's a real problem in academia.

JUDY

Yes, and while I appreciate Gene's confidence in me, not finishing was a possibility that loomed large in my mind, if only because I'd seen it happen to so many (brilliant) friends and acquaintances. So I appreciated Ray giving me that stern directive. It strengthened my spine.

Ray's second instruction was scarier. It was that I needed to make two phone calls. "You need to call the man who owns the property up at Arrowhead. Let him know that you are trying to raise the money to purchase this for the kingdom of God, for pastors and missionaries. Let him know what God is doing.

"And you also need to call the man whose name God gave you on the first night of your vision. Let him know that God started the vision with his name."

That was terrifying enough, right? Call up two strangers out of the blue—and not just strangers, but strangers who were successful, powerful men who likely had little time for impertinent demands from a shoestring ministry?

GENE

But Ray didn't leave it at that. Next, he said, "Then you need to make even more phone calls." He told us that he wanted us to call "anybody who is somebody" and ask them to support the vision.

He wasn't being a snob by saying "anybody who is somebody." Not at all. He was reflecting the truth that in order to gather supporters, we first needed to gather proven leaders.

We needed the endorsement of people who had two important qualifications: 1) they saw a need for what we were doing, and, 2) they were people that other people already trusted.

Judy

Yes, this instruction of Ray's, though it was intimidating, was so very, very wise. As he spoke, I began to realize just how significant his voice was going to be in getting our fledgling ministry off the ground.

Gene

He had wisdom far beyond what we had at the time, and it was wisdom that had grown out of his own vast experience. He had spent many years observing how God moves when creating something He desires to have exist in His world.

Ray—and everyone else in that tiny meeting room—saw the need so clearly. They saw the pastors on the ground who were working hard for God, but whose hearts were empty.

Judy

Yet it was hard to jump from the need we all saw and into the action required to meet the need. I'll be frank: all three things that Ray instructed us to do felt like tall orders.

But he didn't just instruct us; he encouraged us. He told us that we needed to be "bold and courageous," and in that moment, I remembered the message I'd heard in chapel from Ann Graham Lotz. It was another echo.

Ann's message—which I hadn't been able to get out of my head the week before the vision—had been all about being bold and courageous. She'd spoken from the book of Jeremiah, where God was instructing Jeremiah to obey without fear.

I hadn't known why that message had resonated with me so strongly, or why the Lord had continued to bring it back into my mind.

But now, listening to Ray, I knew.

God had given me that message because He'd known I was going to need it.

GENE

Yes, Judy needed it, because the people she was getting ready to contact were famous and powerful within Christian circles. She was going to contact everyone from Lloyd Ogilvie, the chaplain of the U.S. Senate in Washington, D.C., to the head of Promise Keepers (a huge and influential evangelical organization), to Chuck Swindoll, pastor at the Evangelical Free Church of Fullerton and a hugely influential author and speaker.

Judy

It felt very strange to be calling all of these people and asking them to endorse a vision that God had given me, with nothing tangible yet to show that the vision was going to become a reality.

I worried over what I was going to say. After all, what *could* I say? "Hi, I'm Judy TenElshof. I'm a professor at Talbot School of Theology at Biola University. God has given me a vision for a renewal center for pastors and Christian leaders, for which there is a great need. And we would like *you* to send us a letter of endorsement!"

No one would listen. No one would believe. And *certainly* no one would send a letter of endorsement.

Or so I thought.

But I was obedient to do it anyway.

I called so many people. So many big names. All of the people that Gene just mentioned above—and also mega-church pastors, like Kenton Beshore of Mariners, and leaders at top organizations like Focus on the Family, and deep thinkers I respected hugely, like philosopher and author Dallas Willard.

It was terrifying. It made my hands shake. It made my voice tremble.

And yet...

And yet, in the end, there was not one single person we asked for an endorsement who did not respond with a resounding, "Yes!"

GENE

It was amazing. It was such an astonishingly unanimous consensus.

All of these people, these great and famous Christian leaders, had the same reaction when they heard what we wanted to do.

All of them said, essentially, *Yes, this is something the church needs.* And, *Yes, we think that you're the ones to do it.*

And, so incredibly, so generously, *Yes, we'll stand behind you. You have our endorsement.*

JUDY

It was a miracle.

It also built my courage—which is a funny thing, when you think about it. I *built* my courage by doing things that *took* courage.

And that was a good thing, because we would need all the courage we could get going forward, especially when it came to contacting the two men who Ray had mentioned to me specifically: the man who owned the property in Arrowhead, and the man whose name God had given me in the vision.

The path ahead seemed to be becoming more and more clear.

But it was also becoming more and more intimidating.

Chapter Six

What the Vision Wasn't

Gene

Even though Hilltop was now a nascent nonprofit, we still had some months to wait after we filed our papers to incorporate as a 501(c)(3). Bureaucracy is slow, and it was going to take some time before everything was finalized.

Meanwhile, we had work to do.

Since Judy had taken on most of the work of contacting all of our endorsers—the people who could back up, with their experience and their name recognition, our claim to be doing something good and needful for the kingdom of God—I took on a very different kind of work.

I took on the research.

Judy

I was so grateful that Gene was willing to shoulder that burden. The nature of my work required me to stay largely near our home, because I had to be in a local classroom most days. I couldn't travel constantly around the States and still fulfill my responsibilities to my students. But Gene's work involved lots of travel, and that gave him a chance not just to research online or through phone conversations, but to actually *visit* retreat centers around the country. He was able to be on the ground, seeing what worked and what didn't.

Gene

Because I wanted that hands-on, real-life experience, the process of research took many months. I was only able to visit these far-flung retreat centers when my company sent me on trips, and of course I had to choose centers that I could reach within the small pockets of time between my scheduled flights and meetings.

But even within those restrictions, I was able to pound a lot of pavement. I visited retreat centers in multiple places—in our own state of California, of course, but also in Washington, Colorado, Michigan, and Wisconsin. Being willing to give myself a long period of time—about half a year—to visit as many retreat centers as I could meant that I was really able to do it right. I was able to get a really good, well-rounded picture of what the current state of American retreat centers was like.

And the answer?

Well, it wasn't pretty.

JUDY

Yes, it became very clear, after Gene's months of travel, that if Hilltop was going to be successful, there were some very common pitfalls that we were going to have to avoid.

GENE

The biggest one? We were going to have to find some way to make sure that our new center didn't sit empty.

It turns out that there are a *lot* of people who want to run retreat centers—and lots of them think God has spoken to them.

But very few of them are actually successful in making their retreat center a going concern. So many of the places I visited just sat empty for the majority of the year.

And it turns out that has nothing to do with cost—it has to do with time. We found that pastors just don't have time to deal with their hearts. Or, at least, they think they don't.

Then they would hit some kind of crisis that knocks them off of their feet and, suddenly, they would find the time to look for help.

JUDY

Yes, it was almost always a disaster that would drive a pastor to seek out a retreat center: it would be either a moral failure or a crisis in the family.

But that kind of emergency care wasn't what we wanted Hilltop to be about. Instead, our vision was to provide a place of safety where the pastors could come and spend some real time alone with God—perhaps a week or more. The reality was that, as things stood, that kind of dedicated time for spiritual growth never happened for most ministers. I found that pastors of my generation didn't get it. They didn't see the need for time alone with God.

So our goal became to reach the *next* generation, which would be students in seminary, and to teach them how to spend time with God and how to pray.

We also wanted to try to reeducate our own generation about the need to open their hearts to what God was doing. They needed to know that whether what was going on was easy or hard, whether it felt good or bad, God was there at work in their hearts.

Gene

Our hope was that having seminarians as one of our primary demographics would solve the problem of keeping the renewal center busy and occupied. Given Judy's connection with Talbot, we knew that if Talbot supported the idea, we could keep the retreat center full during the times when it wasn't being used by the staff of various churches or by missionaries who were home on furlough.

Judy

It wasn't that there was a preexisting demand for a retreat center on Talbot's behalf. It was more that they were open to the idea and, over time, were growing in their acceptance for the need for spiritual formation for their students.

The faculty and staff at Talbot really loved their students, and that was why they were willing to listen to new approaches to student health and flourishing—and that's really what the idea of spiritual formation was seen as in evangelical circles at the time: something new, but something that might be promising.

In many ways, the school was being led by God to take risks and step out into new areas of exploration. I think that God was growing their hunger for spiritual formation at the same time that He was developing Hilltop. They were hesitant, at times, but we were passionate in presenting what we saw as a necessity. Those years were hard, I'll admit, but to their credit, folks at the school were willing to listen and experiment, and all of us went into the conversations with a lot of trust and faith—both in God and in each other.

There was a lot that my team did to get the buy-in from Talbot. We met with professors and let them experience what the students did by having them do life maps in groups of ten or so. This formed an immense amount of closeness and community among the faculty. We also met with five of our leading theologians and developed the biblical and theological foundations of spiritual formation that Dr. Robert Saucy authored. This treatise is now read by all the students at the beginning of their programs.

We also had retreats with the faculty and students up in Big Bear—another location in the San Bernardino mountains—where the faculty served the students. Everyone, faculty and students, went into the woods with their Bibles and spent time in solitude, silence, and prayer. Then they'd come back together and discuss what their experience was like and share communion together.

Acceptance of the necessity of investing in spiritual formation didn't come easily at Talbot; there was lots of foundation work that had to be done. But the Lord did the work. The work was slow to our eyes maybe, but it was sure, certain, and firm—the kind of work that lasts.

Gene

In the end, we had a seminary that wanted such a place to send their seminarians, and that wanted their seminarians to have the sort of training in spiritual formation and prayer and solitude that we intended to offer. That meant, in terms of Hilltop, that we were starting with a leg up. In some ways, we were going to be filling a need instead of being forced to create a demand.

And as anyone who's ever done any kind of marketing at all would be willing to tell you, that's a huge advantage.

Judy

The other thing that Gene found out was that part of the reason there was such a demand was because we were Protestants—evangelicals.

It turned out, as he did his cross-country research, that there *were* some places you could find the sort of Spirit-centered, preventative-care-oriented retreats that we had envisioned. That was at Roman Catholic retreat centers.

For Protestant evangelicals, however, this type of renewal center was nowhere to be found.

Gene

Yes. This was a place where our Catholic brothers and sisters were ahead of us. I appreciated their good example, and I wanted us to have the same sort of resource available to our own ministers and missionaries. It's important that pastors seeking the kind of rest and refreshment we wanted to offer would be able to be found in a place where they were theologically comfortable. The renewal center at Arrowhead that we wanted to build would offer a place where nothing would get in the way of these ministers spending time with God. Even though ecumenical discussions—and even legitimate arguments!—are well-worth having, and can be both clarifying and faith-affirming, they would be distracting to the kind of peace and solitude we wanted pastors to experience at Hilltop.

We wanted Hilltop to be a place where nothing would be in the way between pastors and God.

Judy

It was important for both of us that we kept that goal in mind: that we focused on the good thing that we knew the Lord wanted to do, and not on all the obstacles that were standing in our way.

It was important to focus on the goal, because otherwise the obstacles would overwhelm us—and the next hurdle to be jumped was now right in front of me.

I had to call the man who owned the property up in Arrowhead.

Gene

The man who owned the property up in Arrowhead was no shrinking violet. He was a man with a big personality… and a big heart to match. He was a well-known philanthropist who cared deeply about God and about his fellow man. But since he's not the sort of man who seeks out public recognition for his good deeds, we want to respect his privacy, so for the purposes of this book, we'll call him "George." George always prayed seriously about the projects he gave to, and he made a practice of waiting on God until he heard Him speak.

He also had an intimidating presence that many people couldn't get past.

Judy

We did have the advantage of knowing some of these things about him before we spoke, mostly because Ray Ortlund had been George's mentor for years and years, but also because our daughter-in-law had been in college with his daughter, and we had met him briefly once, when he had picked his daughter up from a ski trip that she had joined our family on.

In some ways, that connection made the prospect of calling George easier—but in some ways it made it harder, both because I knew enough about George to find him intimidating and also because I really, really didn't want to disappoint Ray.

Also, just like with the people we asked for endorsements, it was hard to figure out what to say. The plain truth just sounded so abrupt, so bold: "God gave us a vision and focused us on your property as the means of carrying it out. We wanted you to know that we are attempting to raise money to purchase your property."

How do you start a conversation like that?

Well, some months went by before I got up the courage to call George. But finally, one day, I found myself with a small space of time in my office before I was due to teach my next class, and I felt the courage to make the call.

To be honest, I thought I would just get a secretary and leave a message—I didn't actually expect to connect to George on the first try. I figured he'd probably just call me back later.

But God planned things differently. Yes, a secretary answered, but she said that George was in, and she transferred the call.

I was so surprised—and then I was even more surprised when I didn't even have to explain who I was or why I was calling! George immediately said that he knew who Gene and I were, and he even knew we'd traveled up the mountain to view his property.

I could tell he was feeling like I was going to ask him for something, but that wasn't really what I was trying to do.

What I *really* wanted to do was just to give him information. I wanted to tell him what God was doing, and then leave it up to him to decide if he wanted to act on that information.

Or not.

"Well," I said, nervous but pressing on, "let me tell you why we did that." And I tried to explain the vision to him.

But George was short with me—not mean or rude, but just very brisk and business-like. "If God *were* speaking to you about my property," he said, "He'd probably be talking to me, too. And He's not."

I replied, "You're probably right."

And that was the end of that conversation.

I put down the phone, my heart sinking. Well, that was it, wasn't it? The man who owned the property I was sure the renewal center was supposed to be on—a man with a reputation for hearing and obeying God's voice—was sure that God was not telling him to support the renewal center.

The vision I'd been carrying in my heart for six months now—the vision that had seemed to be miraculously confirmed time and again—that vision?

It was dead.

Gene

Every journey has its setbacks, and this was a big one. First there had been the results of my research trips across the States, when I had visited empty center after empty center. It was so disheartening, and had led me to a horrible-but-inevitable question: why go to all the work and trouble and expense of building yet another empty shell? Could this really be what God wanted?

And now our hopes of the house up in Arrowhead were just like all those sad retreat centers: empty and abandoned. The tour of the retreat centers had been a sort of wearing, subtle discouragement; the phone call with George was a more direct, abrupt disappointment.

Nothing was turning out the way we expected.

JUDY

The truth was—though we wouldn't see it till much later—that God was not done teaching us how He shapes visions. Everything was going to happen according to His timeline, not ours.

In the end, even these discouraging setbacks played their part in refining the way the vision would come to life.

But on the day of the phone call, I couldn't see any of that. I was depressed, disheartened—just plain old *sad.* The last thing I wanted to do was to go and stand up in front of a class of young, faith-filled, energetic students.

But that was my job, and so that's what I went and did.

And as He so often does, God surprised me by meeting me in the course of my ordinary, day-to-day duties.

As I arrived at the class, I knew that I couldn't hide my sadness from my students and, anyway, I never wanted to lie to them or be deceptive towards them. So I told them the truth. I said, "There's something I've been working on for six months—a vision that I'm sure that the Lord gave me. But it's just fallen flat. All those six months of work disappeared today. Just like that."

Then, in a cheery segue that I was far from feeling, I said, "And I'm sure I'm not the only one in need of prayer today! Let's start class by breaking up into groups and praying for each other's prayer requests."

As the groups formed, I joined one of them. In our seminary context, this kind of devotional activity wasn't out of place—it was part of why all these students were here.

When I sat down with my chosen group, one of the undergrad students piped up. "Professor TenElshof," she said, "visions usually die and come back several times while coming into being. That's how God shapes them."

Wow! The student didn't know it, but those words spoke healing straight into my tired heart. It was another Holy Spirit moment: God directing His words to me, using the means of another person of faith.

In that moment, I knew that God was not only good, but that He wanted me to *know* His goodness. He wanted me to know that He would continue to lead me as I continued to walk in faith.

He would lead me into the moment when the vision would become reality.

Gene

Visions die and then they come back reshaped. That student could have no idea what her words would mean to us going forward. They would become a life-preserver in the days to come.

Judy

A life-preserver we would need! Because despite all the work that we'd done so far, I still haven't mentioned the other task on the list that Ray had given me: talking to the man whose name God had given me in the first place.

It was another hurdle in the race and jumping over it was going to take a great deal of faith.

Chapter Seven

A Year-to-Date Confirmation

Judy

During the same fall season that I had my conversation with the owner of the Arrowhead house, I also followed Ray Ortlund's third instruction: I talked to the man whose name God had given me on the night of the vision: Jim Hamel.

But that conversation didn't require me to gather up my courage and make a cold call, like I'd done with George.

Instead, this time, God brought the man to me.

It was October, and I was walking across Biola's campus. It felt like an ordinary day—which is how most extraordinary days feel, right up until the unexpected happens.

That day, all of the sudden, as I was going about my ordinary business, I found myself face-to-face with Jim, and, of course, the first thing that popped into my head is, *Ray said I have to tell Jim about the vision.*

I hadn't done it yet, but like I said, when someone as wise as Ray Ortlund gives you marching orders, *of course* you're going to follow them. So here I was, suddenly in a position to do what Ray had asked me to do—and I had no time at all to think about what I was going to say!

So I said the first thing that came to my mind. I asked Jim, "Do you believe in visions?"

If I'd had time to prepare, I'm sure I wouldn't have started with such a blunt question!

But, to my surprise, he said, "Yes, I actually do."

Then, to my further surprise, he asked *me* a question. He asked, "Do you want to hear about the vision that God gave to me?"

Gene

One of the interesting things about Jim was that, though at the time Judy talked to him, he was a very successful businessman, he hadn't started out in life with a silver spoon in his mouth. Not by a longshot. He'd started as a guy who didn't have the proverbial two dimes to rub together.

And, it turned out, it was at that time in his life—the time before he'd made any real money—that the Lord chose to share something with him in a vision.

Judy

Of course my answer to Jim's question, "Do you want to hear about the vision God gave to me?" was an emphatic, *Yes, I'd love to!*

So he told me. He said that, back in the days before he'd had any of his big financial successes, God had sent him a dream. In that dream, God showed him a big, palatial house, filled with many fireplaces, and each of those fireplaces was spewing out money.

God told him that all of the money was going to be his, and that he was going to use it to care for people.

I listened to him attentively, and could not help but think, *Wow, I* have *to share my vision with him.* He was so honest and forthright with me; I wanted to treat him just as earnestly and sincerely—no matter how nervous I was!

So I told him that God had given me a vision, and I told him that the vision had started with his name.

He listened to me in turn, but when I finished sharing, he stayed silent. It was the kind of silence that felt like it could last and last.

Finally, I spoke up again. I said, "You know, what you do with what I've told you is between you and God. I just wanted to be faithful to God to share it with you."

And with that, we parted ways.

Gene

What we had no idea of, at the time, were the strange ways Jim's vision of the fireplaces would echo forward into the future. Hilltop's history, as it turned out, was going to involve fire and flames and ashes, in a very true, literal, and traumatic way.

It was also going to involve God bringing beauty out of those ashes.

But all of that was way in the distance ahead of us, and we had no idea it was coming.

Judy

No, at the time all we knew was: *Nothing is happening.*

They say it's darkest before the dawn, but some dark nights last longer than a mere twelve hours. At this point, it felt like we had been waiting in the gloom for almost half a year.

We'd incorporated, we'd had that initial burst of support and enthusiasm from others, and then…nothing.

What did we do? Well, what *could* we do? We just continued our normal work. That was the only answer. Gene kept working in the business world, and I kept on teaching at the seminary.

Looking back on that time—and at some of the times that followed—I think what was going on, without my realizing it, was that God was taking the time to grow in me the kind of faith and prayer life He wanted me to then pass on to others. He wanted me to trust Him in the dark of nothing happening.

At Hilltop, we were going to be asking people to be intimate with God, to be spiritually naked before Him. No barriers. Nothing held back. Alone. In solitude. Just them and God.

And to be able to help people enter into that kind of closeness with the Lord, to have the faith that He would meet them there, God had to grow that same kind of faith in me first.

I think that's why the vision took so many years to come about. God had to work a deep level of faith in me, and I had to learn how to simply *be* with God—in the same way that we would eventually, at Hilltop, ask others to *be* with God.

But, at the time, I couldn't see that.

I was just in the dark, struggling to keep putting one foot in front of the other, with no idea how the promise would eventually come to pass.

At work, I'd pass my dean, Dennis Dirks, in the hall, and he'd asked me, "Anything yet?" He meant, *Has the ministry received any money yet?* Remember, he was on our newly-established board—the board of this *non-profit* that was currently *non-funded* as well!

So, he would ask me, "Anything yet?" and I would always have to answer, with a small smile, a shake of my head, and as much hope as I could muster, "Not yet. But maybe tomorrow!"

Those repeated conversations were always a reminder of one thing: that even the vital first step of buying a property (let alone furnishing it and running it as a retreat center) was still way out of our reach.

I hated that I always had to answer, "No."

Gene

It was a time of waiting, to be sure. Though, I'll be honest, at that point, the ministry was still weighing heavier on Judy's mind than on mine. I'd done what I could, and then I put it down until there was something else for me to do.

JUDY

I think that's true! It was another way we complemented each other: we approached problems and tasks differently. I appreciated the way Gene could, as they say, *Let go and let God.*

I was more the sort to say, "God, I'm letting this go into your hands...but could I have an update, please?"

GENE

Very true! And if Judy appreciates my calmness, I appreciate her perseverance. I know she spent those long, gloomy months in constant prayer. God had given her a promise, and she was not going to let it go!

JUDY

No, I didn't let it go...but I did doubt. I have to be truthful about that. It was continuing to walk forward, in the midst of that doubt, that the Lord used to help grow my faith.

So, there we were, months past any kind of movement on the project. Dennis would pass me in the hall, ask, "Anything yet?" and I'd be forced—one more time—to say, "No."

And then, because I just couldn't bear to admit defeat, I'd force myself to add, "But maybe tomorrow!"

Not that I believed it.

Days passed. Weeks passed. Months passed.

Until, finally, a whole year passed. It was February again—February 19, 1997, to be exact. It was a year to the day after the first night of my vision and it seemed an ordinary Wednesday, like any other.

Walking through my normal, quotidian routine, trying to ignore the significance of the date, I went to the mailbox and opened my mail.

And there, unbelievably, was a check.

It was for the renewal center. It was for $10,000.

And it was from Jim: the man whose name God had given me on the first night of the vision.

CHAPTER EIGHT

STRENGTH FOR THE JOURNEY

JUDY

With that first major donation from Jim—that $10,000 check I received exactly one year after God first gave me the vision—we were finally able to begin real work on the project.

Our official incorporation papers arrived about a month after Jim's check, and, with that, *Hilltop Renewal Center* was officially born.

GENE

Yes, the work began in earnest—and it truly proved to be a busy year! Since we were officially a nonprofit organization, the Board of Directors was able to meet for the first time with representatives from all three supporting ministries present (CRM, PRM, and TIM).

Judy

It was an unreal moment to be there, with all of these men supporting us, knowing that through them, their organizations were supporting us also. God had done an amazing work already, just getting us all together in that room.

That first $10,000 donation let us, as a Board, get started conducting business. Given that Jim, our first major donor, happened to be a printer who was generous not just with his money but also with his time and resources, even ordinary business tasks like printing brochures, stationary, and envelopes proved to be a joy. Each new piece of printed material was a reminder of how God had provided for us.

The $10,000 wasn't the millions we needed to buy the property, but it was more than anyone had ever given us before, and when I opened that check, I thought, *Wow, someone else believes in this. God is moving in other people's hearts too, granting them the desire to give to this vision.*

Gene

Putting together that first real brochure was a defining moment—and I mean that literally. In deciding which words we were going to use to describe our project, we were giving a *definition* to the name "Hilltop Renewal Center." Jim's company lent us their expertise in making our printed materials look good, but it was up to us to make sure the words on the page were accurate—that they really described the mission God had set before us.

Here is some of how we saw our mission at the time:

Hilltop will provide facilities, grounds, lodging, food, and various support personnel for people interested in quiet, solitude, study, and spiritual direction, as well as group interaction that supports these activities.

Because of this focus, Hilltop will not invest in or develop the various amenities that are customary in conference centers that seek to provide entertainment and outdoor activities for guests.

Instead, Hilltop will seek property that is well-suited to seclusion and quiet, in an atmosphere that invites communion with God and spiritual renewal.

Shawn Hofer, a friend of ours from Colorado who later helped give shape to the Intentional Character Development Program at Talbot School of Theology, helped us create a logo that fit our mission. He worked and worked on that logo until he got it exactly right, and then he generously donated it—his intellectual property—to the ministry, to use however we liked in perpetuity. We put it on our new stationary, our envelopes, everything! It's still the same logo we use today.

If this all sounds like a lot of paperwork...well, it was. And I haven't even gotten into all the legal forms and the like.

I also have to praise Jim: after that first substantial gift of $10,000, and his help with all of our printed materials, he continued to keep up his support of the ministry. Over the years, when the ministry was in need of money, Jim would often make new donations to Hilltop, usually with gifts of $25,000 at a time.

But those years of ministry were still ahead of us. That first year was different. To put it simply: the year after we incorporated was the year we worked on infrastructure.

Judy

It was also the year that I finally finished following all of Ray Ortlund's original instructions to me. How? By finishing my PhD.

That's right—no "All But the Dissertation" for me! I was now Dr. TenElshof, with my doctorate in Marital and Family Therapy from Fuller Theological Seminary, along with a corresponding second masters, this time in theology.

With those degrees now in hand, I presented my new plan for pastor care to Dennis Dirks, my dean. The plan was designed to help pastors deepen their walks with God, maintain and grow their intimacy with God and with their families, and relate with integrity to the members of their churches. The program, as I first envisioned it, would begin when the pastors-to-be entered seminary, and would continue after graduation with the alumni.

The dean heard me out and, even though he cautioned me that my plan was very ambitious, and was worried that the program might be grounded too much in psychology and not be ministry-oriented enough, he *did* let me begin it—with one class.

Gene

The dean's willingness to give this new thing a try spoke really well of him, I think. And, he didn't just dip a toe into the waters. Instead, Dennis took a place on Hilltop's board and has been a big and wonderful part of this ministry, and of other efforts at pastor care.

But it shows how much our culture still has to learn about spiritual development, even if you're a devout, active, caring Christian. People don't know, simply because they haven't been taught. They don't know that it takes *prevention* to keep from falling away from God. That going on retreat, seeking God in solitude—all of that is important to do when you feel like things are going well. It's not something to turn to only when things have fallen completely apart.

Think of it this way: in order to have a good marriage, you want to spend deliberate time with your spouse on a regular basis. Can therapy and marriage retreats and stuff like that help save a dying marriage? Sure, if both people are on board. But why let it get to that state in the first place? Isn't it better to spend that marriage retreat with a spouse you actively love, actively *like,* and really know? Of course!

In the same way, it's also better to actively and deliberately keep your relationship with God strong. Just like you would with a spouse or a friend. Tend to the healthy relationship, so you don't end up sitting beside your dying relationship like you would beside a hospital sickbed.

JUDY

Yes, everything Gene just laid out was so important for us to keep in mind as we worked on the ministry's infrastructure that year—especially because that was also a year that had its share of testing and trials. One came in the fall, when we decided to attend the National Caregivers Conference, in order to meet others who were running retreat centers across the country.

This conference was held in Colorado Springs, a beautiful location, right up next to the Rocky Mountains. Mostly, I found there the same problem that Gene had found elsewhere: most retreat centers and caregivers were oriented towards helping people in crisis rather than being focused on preventative care. And most were desperately looking for people to fill their centers.

To tell the truth, being around so many people who were focused on helping those in crisis made me doubt our mission a bit. Looking back, that temptation to doubt was just that: a temptation. I was still growing in my ability to have faith—to *keep* the faith—regarding what God had so clearly shown me.

But it was also at this conference that I met a couple who ran a retreat center in the Midwest; I'll call them Lois and Virgil, though those aren't their real names. To put it simply, we hit it off! I felt like we were connecting in a meaningful way. I felt that they shared our mission and I began to hope that our new Hilltop ministry might be able to partner with these people.

After the conference, Lois and Virgil came out to California, to meet with me and some other folks from Talbot. It was at that meeting that a colleague was able to see what I could not: this couple wasn't really interested in supporting our mission. They were looking to use our connections for themselves.

I couldn't see it, but my colleague could. I didn't have eyes to see it, but he did. I'm thankful for that—for him! I truly am. God used him to protect our fledgling ministry.

But…

While I was grateful to my fellow professor for helping me see what was really going on, I found myself crying after that meeting. Here I had thought I'd found peers for me and for Gene—people who could understand the work we were doing and who would walk beside us in it.

Instead, it was just someone looking for an advantage. I was heartbroken.

As God continued to lead us, we often felt the way the Israelites must have felt as they wandered in the wilderness: lost and alone. But God never stopped being faithful in giving to the Israelites out of the abundance of His own goodness. And He did the same for us. Like it says in Deuteronomy 1:30-31:

> The LORD your God, who is going before you, will fight for you, as he did for you in Egypt, before your very eyes, and in the wilderness. There you saw how the LORD your God carried you, as a father carries his son, all the way you went until you reached this place.

We truly needed God's strength for the journey.

GENE

Yes, we needed His strength to stay faithful to His calling.

Faithfulness is not always exciting. Very often, it looks like the simple act of putting one foot in front of another and continuing to walk along the path to which you've already committed yourself.

JUDY

That's right. And even though continuing to walk forward, step by step, is an ordinary—sometimes even boring!—action, God often uses our walking forward in faith to bring us around the corner and into the sight of the cool waters of refreshment that our hearts were longing for.

And so it proved again, in our lives. When I was feeling so very low, God brought encouragement to me through the ordinary means of my work as a professor.

As 1998 was nearing its end, we had done all that we had been told to do, and were simply waiting. We had listened, we'd prayed, we'd talked to people...and now it was time to wait.

Waiting was grueling.

Even after everything we'd done, we couldn't do more without money—and a lot of money, at that! $3.2 million was what we needed in order to buy the Hilltop property up in Arrowhead. *$3.2 million.* Just pennies to God, as I'd told Gene, but still...it was a lot of money to us.

Since we'd done such a good job of telling everyone about the vision and about the ministry, I had people asking me often about our progress. Day after day, asking me if there was news.

And I'd always have to say, "No."

It was getting very hard to have to say, "no," over and over and over again.

One day in particular, I remember being very tired of people asking how we were going to raise the money and how long it was going to be before the vision became a reality. I got up that morning and said to God, "I need you to confirm the vision today, or I am done waiting." I was so tired of looking foolish, tired of looking naive in my belief that God would provide millions of dollars for a vision He'd given me.

I know this admission doesn't make me look like any kind of a super-believer, but that's just the point: I want people to know how God works through us, even in our weaknesses. He's so kind! He loves us as we are, and He meets us there, and He helps us to grow. It's very important to me to share honestly about the sequence of miracles that God led us through and the way He kept our hope alive.

Whenever I felt like giving up hope, God would send another sign.

So it was that day. I started the morning full of doubt, telling the Lord I was at the end of my rope: He needed to confirm the vision that day, or my grip was going to slip. (There's a lot to be said for being honest in front of God! After all, He knows the truth about you already anyway.)

I started the morning in doubt, but I still got up, got dressed, and went about my normal work.

In the ordinary course of my job as a professor, I often met with and listened to and counseled people who were in need of a mentor's ear. One of those people, that day, was Kathleen Doyle, a resident director (RD) at Biola, who was facing some transitions and wanted to ask my advice. I agreed, and we met together at a free lunch that was being put on that day by the Associated Student Body at tables they'd set up on a cool green lawn dotted with sycamores.

There, under the shade of those giant trees, I listened and advised, and then listened some more. But, as I listened, I began to feel the Holy Spirit prompting me to share the vision with Kathleen.

I argued with myself internally—I was supposed to be here serving this young woman; why would I hijack the conversation towards my own concerns?

But the prompting continued and so, at an appropriate break in the conversation, I shared what was on my heart.

And as Kathleen responded, I was met once again with an astonishing, miraculous coincidence: it turned out that not only did Kathleen have friends who were friends of George, the property owner up in Arrowhead, but Kathleen herself had been up on the property just the weekend prior!

Kathleen said that as she was walking the property with George and his wife, the wife mentioned that there was a buyer for the property who was interested in purchasing it and then dividing up the acreage and building three different homes on the property! But George's wife didn't want to see the property divided, and so they wouldn't sell it.

As Kathleen spoke, I knew that God had sent her as an answer to my morning request for confirmation. In her words,

I heard God affirming the vision and showing me that He was holding the property for the purpose He'd declared to me. He never let my faith waver for more than twenty-four hours.

He was so good.

Chapter Nine

Provisions for the Way

Gene

It was January of 1999, and almost two years since God had given Judy the vision. She and I continued to think about the property up in Arrowhead, but the large sums of money that would be needed to buy it were not coming into the coffers of our new nonprofit.

Judy

Yes, as time went by, it seemed that nothing was happening.

Then, one January day, out of the blue, we got a phone call from George, the owner of the property.

I was so surprised! Somehow, despite that, I got through the normal courtesies at the beginning of the call: *Hello, how are you, doing fine, thanks…*

Then George got to the meat of the call. He asked about Hilltop and about how our fundraising was going for the project.

I told him that while several other ministries had joined us, and the number of supporters we had was growing, we still didn't have anything close to the amount of money that we needed in order to purchase his property.

To my further surprise, he didn't answer this sorry bit of news with the equivalent of, *Oh well, gotta go,* but instead he said that God was now speaking to him about our ministry. He asked if Gene and I would be willing to meet him for lunch.

"Of course!" I said. I was excited at his interest in the renewal center, but still confused and in the dark about how he might want to be involved given that we were...well...some several *million* dollars short of our goal.

Nonetheless, we made plans to meet him at his home on Lido Isle in Newport Beach, and then I hung up the phone.

I was burning with curiosity about what God was going to do next—what new twist would this lunch meeting bring?

But, of course, I had to wait for the day of our appointment.

GENE

Newport Beach, where George lived, is a gorgeous bit of land. It's a place where the shoreline of the Pacific Ocean wanders in and out of a large bay. The southwestern part of the city is full of large, exquisite homes, and the back bay up towards the northeast is a nature preserve—a true wildlife sanctuary—full of sandbars, hardy grasses, and waterfowl. Everywhere you go in Newport, you can smell the tang of the saltwater, and feel the freshness of the wind off of the ocean. It's a beautiful place.

We met George at his home on the shore. It was a beautiful home on a large corner lot, overlooking where the bay flowed into the ocean. After walking around his property and making small talk, he invited us to walk an easy distance with him, out of the residential area, and over to a restaurant called the Blue Water Grill. The restaurant's windows looked out over the boats docked at the marina.

JUDY

Once we had been seated and had given our orders to the waitstaff, George began to tell us why he'd asked us there today.

It was because he'd had a conversation with God.

George said that one day in prayer, he'd asked God why his property, Hilltop, was not selling. He said that God answered, "Because Hilltop belongs to Me."

George then argued with God and listed some of the many ways that he had served the Lord and had been generous with his money. "I give liberally. I've done this, this, and this for you."

God then told him, "But everything you have belongs to Me."

So George told God, "Okay. You can have Hilltop.

"And that," George concluded, "is why I felt I needed to call you."

It was astonishing to listen to him. I sat there, my heart full of wonder at this unexpected turn of events.

Gene

But then something else unexpected happened. George looked at us, and he said, "You know, I'm not sure Hilltop is the property you should have for your vision. So I want to talk to you a little about that."

That was a sharp turn in the course of the conversation! And we didn't even get a chance to ask him more about it, because immediately after he said that, he excused himself to the restroom, leaving Judy and me alone at the table.

I turned to Judy, full of puzzlement. "What do you make of that?" I asked.

"I don't know," she answered. "But I can't wait to see what comes next!"

Judy

The truth was, I found it confusing that George didn't think his property would be perfect for our purposes after all of these miraculous signs, and also after the conversation where the Lord told him, explicitly, "Hilltop is mine." It seemed very clear to me!

But, looking back on it, I think that the Lord chose George to be a part of His project not merely because he had a lot of tangible resources, but also because George had a lot of wisdom about how to accomplish big projects. As it turned out, George was obeying the Lord by not just being generous with his financial resources, but also by being generous with the intelligence, skill, and know-how he'd gained over the years.

His experience was, for him, a sort of sixth sense. It slowed him down and prompted him to look at the big picture. He was absolutely committed to obeying God, but he wanted to obey God wisely, carefully—and honestly. He was right to do that, because wisdom is a gift of God in the first place!

Gene

When George returned to our table, he had a smile on his face. He said, "You'll never guess who's sitting outside on the patio!"

Judy and I looked at each other, but of course we had no idea who he'd run into, so we turned back to George with looks of expectation.

"Ray and Anne Ortlund!" said George.

Ray Ortlund. Our board member, the man who'd given Judy her marching orders—and the man who was also George's long-time mentor.

Judy

Ray and Anne had been up on the Hilltop property in the past, and of course were completely involved in our ministry plans. So I believe that God placed them there, on the restaurant patio, to encourage George to be faithful to what God was telling him to do. I think they were there just to hold George in his firmness of purpose concerning what he was about to say to us.

And what he said was, "I think we should throw a fleece out to God."

In saying that, he was referring to the famous story in the biblical book of Judges where Gideon, one of the Lord's followers, asked the Lord to confirm the instructions He had sent to Gideon by two miracles. In the first miracle, Gideon laid a fleece out on the ground overnight, and asked the Lord to make the fleece wet and the ground all around it dry. In the second miracle, he asked for the opposite: for the ground to be sopping wet and for the fleece to be dry as a bone.

God graciously performed both miracles, confirming that His message to Gideon had been true.

George went on to say that the Hilltop property had been on the market for over two years and was just not selling. But he also said that he felt that Hilltop was not the property we should use for the renewal center because it needed a lot of repair and could become a money pit. This is where George's wisdom and experience came in—he was able to look at the property, and visualize its future. He could see how it might absorb donation after donation into needed repairs without ever becoming the sturdy, usable property that our ministry needed.

That, he said, was why he was proposing that we give a fleece to God. George suggested that he leave the property on the market for its current price, which was $3.2 million and, if it sold, he would give us a half million dollars to start the renewal center elsewhere. On the other hand, if we could raise a million dollars ourselves, he would match that million and the property would be ours.

GENE

To tell the truth, we were ecstatic when we heard this. It was a win-win. Either we'd get a million and the house, or a half million and a fresh start. We couldn't lose! It would be amazing either way.

JUDY

Yes, and we praised God for His kindness. In that moment, it was clear God was going to actually put feet onto this vision and make it a reality.

With His help, we were actually going to do this!

GENE

It was an especially big moment for me. It was the moment I got this sneaking suspicion that maybe this was all actually going to happen. I mean, I'd been faithful in following through on my commitment to the project. I'd done the work. I'd supported Judy.

But after that conversation with George, my attitude began to change. I thought, *This is unreal. Nothing like this has ever happened in my life. This is truly of God.*

And that wasn't even the end of it—the testing of the fleece was still to come.

JUDY

After we finished eating, we left the restaurant by walking past the patio and we found that Ray and Anne were still out there. They stood up and we all greeted each other with hugs.

Then Ray asked George if he'd given us the Hilltop property, and I answered for him. "No," I said, "but he has been *incredibly* generous."

We went home that night conscious of the fact that we'd just seen God working in a mighty way. It was hard to believe what had happened.

And yet there was more to come.

Gene

So we got home and then, *within two weeks*, George's Hilltop property sold for full list.

It had been on the market for two years, and then it sold—for full price, no less!—within *two weeks* of him putting out this fleece before God!

Once it was sold, George was good to his word. He sent us a check right away.

When we got that check for a half a million dollars, I was close to speechless. I'll admit it: that was when it became real to me. I'd had an inkling of what a big deal this was in the restaurant, when I'd thought, *This is unreal...this is truly of God.*

But when I stood there, with an actual, physical check in my hands, and I looked at that huge number on that tiny little slip of paper, I thought, *Oh my gosh, we have to stop talking about Hilltop and actually DO something.*

Back when it had all started, when Judy came home from that conference and said, *I had a vision and I'm supposed to talk to this guy*, I didn't take it as seriously as maybe I should have. I was like, "Oh, that's nice, honey."

I mean, I went along with it...but I was really just going along to get along. My head was still in the corporate world. I had my own life, and the focus of that life was my work. I'd support Judy in her goals—any day, every day, no question—but that's not where my mind was at, you know? That's not where my focus was.

It changed when we got that check for a half million dollars. Once I saw that, I thought, *This is the real deal. Now we have to stop talking about it. Now we actually have to do something.*

It got really real for me in that moment.

Really real...and more than a little scary.

Judy

Adding to the intimidation factor was one more thing: George put a condition on his gift. His stipulation was that we had to use the money within five years, or he wanted it back to give to another organization. He did not want his gift to just sit there idle. He wanted it to be *used* for the kingdom of God.

George was quite a character, but the deepest, most true thing about him is that he's a servant of God. He saw his resources as God's resources, and so when God told him to give, he obeyed. And when he obeyed, he followed through, because he didn't want any of God's resources to be wasted.

I still tear up when I think about the day we got that half million dollar check from George, because it was such an amazing gift—and such a weighty responsibility! To be trusted with that...well, to say that we felt blessed and honored would be an understatement.

My friends and colleagues at Biola and Talbot couldn't quite believe it. *I* still couldn't quite believe it. Because miracles are exciting, and they're scary, and they're so far beyond anything we could do in and of ourselves.

So now we had this money, but we had no place to spend it. The renewal center was now a potential reality, and it was clear that our next step was to look for an appropriate property.

Gene

It was January of 1999 when that original Hilltop property sold, and George sent us that half-million-dollar check. I can understand why George put a time requirement on that much money—that's not chump change.

But we didn't know if we'd be able to fulfill his condition. Either we opened the renewal center within five years, or we had to give the money back.

The clock was ticking. It was time to get it done…or to give it up.

Chapter Ten

Is This the One?

Gene

After we received that half-million-dollar check from George, our first duty was clear: we had to search for the property that would become home to our new ministry.

Judy

We were filled with astonishment, elation, and joy. And we *did* take time to marvel at what had happened, and to praise God for His bounteous provision. But we knew that we couldn't waste time just luxuriating in happy emotions—instead, we took all the energy that our joy gave us and used it for forward momentum on the project itself.

Something else had happened in the meantime to give us a little more of a push forward: Talbot seminary was given a $1.2 million grant from Eli Lilly. My colleagues and I had applied for it together, and it was a five-year grant intended to further spiritual formation in theological education. It included everything we had dreamed of doing for our Talbot students *and* it included resources for our alumni. We now had abundant provisions for our plans to help our students grow in their relationships with God and in their ability to have healthy relationships with their spouses and parishioners.

As I mentioned earlier, my team and I had spent a lot of time at Talbot working to introduce the practices of spiritual formation, through retreats, theological study, and more. This grant rested on that work and it truly felt like the flowering of that work.

If everything went well, Hilltop would eventually become an important part of this grant-funded program: it would be the place where students could, in the course of their schooling, spend serious time in solitude, prayer, and developing intimacy with other students as they shared the work of God in each other's lives.

My dean, Dennis Dirks, said, upon reception of the Lilly grant, "Wow, we've never received this kind of money before!" He named the new program *Segue*, as it was a segue from seminary into the ministry God was calling them into. He gave the student portion over to me to direct, and he gave the alumni portion (and the overall headship) to Mick Boersma. Mick and his wife, Rolanne, had a deep and loving commitment to those from seminary who had chosen ministry as their vocation. They kept up with alumni through a newsletter which they shared with the faculty, and they also took time to visit alumni in other states and countries. Our alumni love Mick and Rolanne and you can see it by the way they stay in touch with them after they leave school. Mick was the perfect person to put in charge of the alumni portion of the new program.

GENE

So, those further developments at Talbot added weight to the responsibility we already felt to move the property search along as quickly as possible. It was clear that we had a window of opportunity open to us—and that it wouldn't stay open forever.

Now we faced the challenge of finding the one property God wanted us to use for His vision from among the hundreds of thousands available in the mountains surrounding Los Angeles—and to find it within the time limit George had given us! But even as we faced this challenge, happily we did *not* face the challenge of finding the perfect person to aid us in our quest.

We already knew a wonderful real estate expert: our son-in-law, Jerry.

JUDY

Jerry had married our daughter, Tami, only a few years earlier, and his family business was real estate. Jerry had caught on to our enthusiasm about the Hilltop project and volunteered to help us find the right property.

It did feel a little odd to be looking for a different property, simply because George's home up in Arrowhead—the one our kids had stayed at and got excited about, the one that had "Hilltop" written above the garage—was the place that had at first seemed God was pointing us towards. It had seemed like *the* place.

Now we had the money, but the place itself was gone. I admit that felt a little strange.

But as I look back on it, I think I can see what the Lord was doing. He said, "Arrowhead," and that's what caused us to consider George's property in the first place. I think that was the point: "Arrowhead" meant we were supposed to *start* there, and by starting there, we were directed to the man who was going to give us the means to launch the ministry. That property also gave us "Hilltop," the name of the ministry. It was about the man and the means and the name, and not about that particular house.

So, again, I was learning about how God works. He has one thing in mind, and you might not know what that one thing is. But as you walk forward in obedience and in faith, God continues to make the way before you clear.

In our case, we followed the instruction to look at Arrowhead, and that's how God provided what we needed in order to start this ministry.

Gene

We began our search by assessing our priorities—formulating our search perimeters. There were certain characteristics that Hilltop's property absolutely needed to have, and foremost among those was the variable that is primary in *any* real estate transaction: *location, location, location.*

Because of what God had told Judy in the vision, we knew that the center was meant to be near Arrowhead. Also, because of our research into what made retreat centers successful, we knew that driving distance mattered. Los Angeles is a big travel hub, and it's easy for folks to fly in. Once they landed at the airport though, they weren't going to want to drive for hours and hours and hours in order to get to the place they were going to sleep that night. We needed the retreat center to be an easy driving distance—both from our main L.A.-area airports and from Biola University itself.

So we drew a large circle around the area, enclosing all the land that was within a two-hour drive from the university.

That was where we'd be looking.

JUDY

The circle we drew represented a big chunk of territory, much of it mountainous. If you take a look at a map of Southern California, you'll see that Los Angeles is situated in a basin between the mountains and the sea. The town of Arrowhead is up in a range to the northeast called the San Bernardinos, which includes Mount San Gorgonio—the highest peak in Southern California.

It's a beautiful area. Driving up there is quite an experience, because after an hour or so of driving through suburb after suburb full of asphalt, concrete, and smog, you suddenly find yourself in rapidly rising foothills that seem to spring up miraculously out of the flat plain. As you climb quickly up the steep and curving road, you soon rise above the smog and you can see the city spread out below you—miles of roads and buildings laid out in a grid-like pattern.

The difference between the smoky-colored air below and the pristine air above is striking.

The hills become mountains and the mountains have their own unique ecosystem. Instead of the numerous palm trees and brilliant fuchsia bougainvillea blossoms that you get in the lowlands, you're surrounded by tall, majestic pines and the white-gray flashes of granite boulders. The sky is so blue, the atmosphere is so clean, and the pure air smells simply delicious.

The San Bernardino mountains are truly a place of beauty and rest.

GENE

The San Bernardino mountains—and the Arrowhead area in particular—were absolutely our target for the new Hilltop property.

But it was hard not to get distracted.

As we began our search, and then as our search dragged on and on, it was easy to get excited anytime anything even *remotely* close to what we were looking for came on the market. The months drifted on, and we still hadn't found what we were looking for. It got to the point where if something was the right size, the right price, and still an easily drivable distance from Los Angeles, we couldn't ignore it.

One such property came up for sale in Temecula, a valley city famous for its vineyards. This property, to be honest, was structured in such a way that it would have made a better summer camp than a retreat center. It was the right price and size and distance, but it wasn't in the mountains, and wasn't really set up the way we wanted.

But it was still the closest thing we'd found so far, and so we put an offer in on it.

JUDY

Honestly, I think we did that because we were beginning to feel desperate. We'd been searching for months and months at this point, and George's five-year clock was really ticking in our heads. If we didn't have a viable ministry going when the time ran out, we'd have to give everything back. George would start a different nonprofit with that money, and the vision for Hilltop would be dead in the water.

What we discovered while we were waiting for the vision to come to pass was that it's really easy to get sidetracked from the purpose God set you running towards. It's easy to begin to develop a vision on your own that is outside of God's plan. After all those years of waiting, we were tempted to start doing things in our own power—trying to make them happen on our own.

GENE

Happily, God saved us from our own overeager impulses! The day—the *very day*—that we made the offer on that large piece of property in Temecula, it was taken off the market. I can't remember what happened to the owner, but it was something dramatic—he died, or traveled off to South America, or something like that. Again, I don't remember quite what it was, but I do remember very clearly thinking, *Well, that's a resounding "no," isn't it!*

It wasn't the only "no" answer, either. We examined and rejected other properties, too—one that comes to mind was a property in the foothills of the San Jacinto mountains, north of Temecula. The problem with that place was that it was on the desert side of the mountains. All of the mountain ranges facing Los Angeles by necessity have one side facing the sea, since Los Angeles sits right on the coast of the Pacific Ocean. That side of the mountains is always pretty green because we get storms coming in off the ocean, and so that side usually gets a decent amount of rain.

The kicker is that the bigger mountain ranges have their other sides facing the desert. And let me tell you, the side of the mountains that faces towards the vast and dry Mojave Desert is *not* as green and pleasant as the side that faces the sea!

The property on the desert side of the mountains was brought to our attention by some Biola friends, and we did go out and look at it, but it didn't feel like it matched up with what God was calling us to do.

But those trips out to various possible properties that *didn't* work made me think hard about what it was that we *did* want. As we visited, the place that kept coming to mind was a particular retreat center I'd visited in Wisconsin as I'd been doing all my research.

That Wisconsin center was one of the few really successful retreat centers I saw during my travels. What stood out about it was two things: it was very well-appointed and it had denominational connections that kept it really full.

So, they took the time, at that center, to furnish the place nicely, to make sure the meals were appetizing and well-cooked. They made sure to execute nicely all the little things that showed attention to detail. And also, because of their connections, they had a constantly full funnel of people wanting to use their facilities.

As we continued our seemingly fruitless search for the perfect property, I kept those two things in mind. That Wisconsin center, for me, served as a reminder of what we wanted to do with Hilltop. There was more to Hilltop's mission than nice appointments and good connections, of course, but, still, I knew those were things that were going to be important to Hilltop's success.

If, that is, we could ever find the right place to build it.

Judy

As Gene said, God closed the door on the property in Temecula that we had put an offer on. But here's the amazing thing. On that same day? God opened a new door, this time in a little place in the San Bernardino mountains called Cedar Pines Park.

Cedar Pines Park not only had the ubiquitous pine trees, it had giant cedar trees—trees so big that they reminded me of those famous California redwoods that are so large that you can't put your arms around their trunks—in fact, it takes many people linking their hands together to encircle them!

And then there were California black oak trees that spread their limbs low enough to make gracious shade for picnickers. These are especially valued as they are nearing extinction.

But the trees that captured my heart at Cedar Pines Park were the dogwoods sprinkled throughout the forest. They created a veil of white lace between the dark pines in the spring, as if the whole forest were celebrating a wedding.

The trees up there captured my heart and were definitely a reflection of the beauty found in the heart of our amazing God.

Jerry was the one who found this new property in Cedar Pines Park in October of 1999. It was a four-story, 8,000-square-foot home, on 57 private acres in the San Bernardino Mountains, with a view of Silverwood Lake, a man-made reservoir very close to Arrowhead.

It was on the market for $750,000 and Gene was sure that price had to be a mistake.

GENE

Yes, it was just too low for such a gorgeous property! You have to understand, even average, run-down, dead-normal small houses in the Los Angeles area had prices creeping towards the half-million-dollar mark. And this huge vacation home was about as far from "dead normal" or "small" as you could get!

The place even had its own well for potable water. The 57 acres it sat on were wooded, and so you could wander around the place in the shade of all these beautiful, mature trees—tall, stately pines and rare black oaks and the quintessential California plant: the redwood. It was like a castle on a hill, with its commanding view of the lake. The home had plenty of bedrooms—five in all. It also had two large rooms that could hold a big group—one on the main floor and one on the second floor at the top of a beautiful, winding staircase. That second-floor room also had a fireplace constructed out of river rocks, quite lovely. The large, modern kitchen featured a walk-in pantry. The third floor could be reached by elevator, and could be used as a library or a dorm, and from it you could access the top floor, which was a glassed-in room that overlooked both the desert, the mountainside, and lake. It was a truly exquisite view during the day, and became even more beautiful at night when you could see the stars.

The structure itself was only ten years old and the whole thing was within easy driving distance of Los Angeles.

It looked like a place that could provide the privacy and luxury of a five-star resort.

If it weren't for...well, let's just say there had been a little bit of neglect in the upkeep.

JUDY

A little! Understatement of the year. We soon found out why it was being offered at such a bargain price. The problems were *huge.*

We understood the state of the property a bit better once we learned more about its history. The property had originally been put on the market for $1.8 million—a price a bit more in keeping with the ridiculously high Southern California real estate market—and so it had taken years for it to drop down to its current price. Still, with Gene's misgivings about it being priced correctly, we had Jerry double-check the listing for us. Sure enough, $750,000 was what was being asked for it now.

It turned out the house had been built by a man for his wife, and after his wife died, the man who owned it walked away from it. The property then reverted back to its original owner, who just wanted it taken off her hands without taking more of a loss. All she wanted was her original investment back.

So, because of all this history, the property had ended up being left vacant for a few years and, well, a lot of little woodland critters had made it their home. Anything that an animal can do to a property, they had done. Also, the pipes had frozen and leaked. It just needed a lot of attention.

Still…everything else was perfect.

We felt like we *had* to make an offer.

So, we offered a little low, and they countered a little higher, and, in the end, we had an offer accepted for a price that was more than fair.

GENE

We did feel like we had to make an offer, but maybe you can see the little hitch in our plans?

That's right: the property was for sale for $250,000 more than we actually had.

Just a little hitch.

So, with George's donation covering about two-thirds

of the price—and remember, we were getting it cheap!—we decided to look into a loan.

There was a bit of a problem with that too: we were a brand-new ministry. We had no track record. We had no credit history.

So, where did that leave us? Well, think about it. Picture me going to the banker—what could I say? "Well, my wife had a vision and we feel God has told us we should have this property and so will you loan us $250,000?"

It makes me laugh just thinking about it!

I know it's funny when I put it that way—I can still picture myself having that conversation, and I would've done it if I'd thought I had no other option—but you can see the problem. We ended up having to go with a private investor.

JUDY

Jerry was the one who was able to connect us with an investor—a businessman who had no particular interest in the retreat center itself, but who had made his fortune by loaning money on projects too risky for big corporate banks. He liked to evaluate projects on a case-by-case basis, and he had a good nose for what was likely to work and what wasn't.

GENE

We took him up to the property and showed him around. On the drive back down to Los Angeles, he asked me a bunch of questions. He was very careful and thoughtful, and I didn't know if he was going to loan us the money or not.

But at the end of the trip, he said, "Okay," and wrote me a check for $250,000.

Judy

We were really grateful to him for loaning us the money we needed, but I'll admit to feeling a bit of unease about the whole thing. After all, God had told me that the ministry was meant to operate debt-free, and now here we were, owing a quarter of a million dollars!

Honestly, looking back, I'd say we still had a lot to learn, at that point, about how to listen to God and how to follow Him. Sometimes we step out on our path, with all the good intentions in the world, we still find ourselves stepping out too quickly—we're hurrying, and we neglect to take the time to really *listen* to God.

In this case, buying the property up at Cedar Pines Park was a quick step, and even though God did say "debt-free," we could see the property was really good for what we wanted to use it for, and really cheap for what we were getting, so we just went ahead and jumped anyway.

It wasn't that we were trying to do the wrong thing. But we hadn't really learned yet how to follow God in a clear way. There was more growth that He still needed to bring about in our lives.

Gene

It really was amazing though. This house—four stories tall, built in the style of a French chateau, set on this beautiful mountainside, close to Los Angeles, and with enough rooms to host a good-sized retreat—this house now belonged to this new ministry we'd started.

It was incredible.

JUDY

It really was. When you walked onto the property, and you saw the beauty of the woods and rocks and sky, it felt like the glory of God in His creation was shouting out to you from every angle.

It was astonishing. It was amazing. It was almost impossible to believe.

Hilltop finally had a home.

Chapter Eleven

A Property, a Community, and a Lot of Elbow Grease

Judy

Even though we had an offer accepted on the Cedar Pines Park property, it took quite a few months to close escrow. During that period of waiting we got what rest we could—because we knew we had a gigantic pile of work waiting for us on the other side!

Gene

And it was a different kind of work than we were used to. When a businessman and a professor say, "We have a lot of work," you picture things that involve paperwork, conversations, meetings, planning, et cetera. And those things were what made up our day-to-day employment, for sure.

But getting the Hilltop property into shape wasn't going to be anything like that. This wasn't a bunch of cerebral, white-collar tasks waiting for us.

This was real, hard, *physical* labor.

Judy

The reason we had so much work in front of us was that the property had sat vacant for over two years. It had pipes that had frozen and burst and that were still leaking. Plenty of mountain critters had made their homes in it. There had even been a person squatting on the property for a while!

There was a well on the property, but it didn't work properly, and figuring out how to get water *up* the hill so that it would stream *down* towards the house with adequate water pressure was a practical physics problem that ate up a lot of time.

Gene

If you've ever house-trained a puppy or had to deal with a rat infestation, you can probably imagine the sort of things we were having to take care of. We had to repair and clean *inside* the house. But it wasn't just the inside of the house that was in trouble.

There was a whole other world of hurt *underneath* the house.

It turned out that the heating structure under the house had been eaten away by opportunistic animals. You wouldn't think that plastic and wire and such would be appetizing to any sort of mammal, but...well, I guess some critters just aren't that picky.

Inside the house, you'd turn the heat on, and it would kind of only half come on. A bit of warm air blew out of the vents, but nothing like what you really needed to actually raise the indoor temperature of a building that size—and this was up on a mountain, at a high elevation, where the winters brought snow and ice. We *needed* the heat to work!

I had the unenviable job of physically wriggling down under the building and wedging myself into the extremely cramped crawlspace. And I stand well over six feet tall, so you can imagine the sorts of pretzel shapes I had to curl myself into!

The crawl space wasn't just cramped, it was dark and smelly too. It was filled with animal droppings, and if you're also imagining spiders and cobwebs and other creepy-crawlies, well, you wouldn't be wrong.

But that's where the damaged ductwork was, and so that's where I had to be.

It's amazing how "glamorous" working for God can get!

Judy

Yes, people talk about "getting their hands dirty" in a project—well, we literally were!

But it was all worth it. At first, I had a hard time imagining the potential of the house, but that changed due to some help from some friends who had a home on Lake Arrowhead. Their home was beautiful and one of them had what I can only call a gift for décor. We invited her to come and take a look at the property, and as she toured through the home, she used her intuitive gift to help me see how the home could be changed, appointed, and decorated to meet the ministry's needs. After her visit, and with her insights in mind, I would walk through that house, and even though there wasn't any furniture, and it was run-down, and not yet fit for anyone to live there, I could still see what it was going to become. That sense of the possibilities gave me the strength to get my hands dirty and get to work.

The bones of that house were so good. It was huge—8000 square feet of floor and four stories tall. It had five separate bedrooms that were each big enough for a couple of people to share, and then a large room near the top that would provide space for single accommodations. There was a beautiful winding staircase inside, but there was also an elevator, which was wonderful when it came to accessibility.

The room at the top of the house was glassed-in, with such a lovely view. At night, you could look right out at the stars—so many of them! We were above the smog and light pollution of the city, and so the whole Milky Way was there, scattered like diamonds across black velvet, the stars twinkling in all their glory.

You just couldn't be in that house without thinking about God, because it was so perfectly built for you to be able to see His creation.

And given that we were preparing the place for people to come up and pray, that was exactly what we wanted.

Gene

I joke about the "glamour" of the work, but honestly, it was a privilege. After walking by faith and not by sight for so many years since the Lord had given Judy the vision for Hilltop, it was so satisfying to finally be doing real work, in the real place where the ministry would begin. It was a massive job, but it was satisfying, and, like I said, it was a privilege.

Judy

We weren't even completely finished with all of the refurbishment before we began hosting retreats there.

Those first retreats were *not* the comfy, cushy experience that Gene had observed in the more successful retreat centers he visited—an experience we hoped to eventually replicate. No, there at the beginning, we had no money—actually, we had less than no money; we were deeply in debt! We scrounged around for lawn chairs and card tables to serve as our furniture, although we didn't even have enough of those at the beginning. I remember people sitting around cross-legged on the rugs on the floor during the first few retreats! And the people who came up found themselves *sleeping* on the floor as well.

Really, it was much closer to camping than it was to anything else.

Eventually, as the ministry started to gain steam, we were able to do a little better. As money came in, we added better furnishings here and there.

But our start was very bare-bones.

Gene

The first folks who came up there were from Talbot, of course. Some of the faculty used it, and that was great, because then they were able to tell their students about it, and to support us and speak well of us in various university settings. Word of mouth is important at the start of any business, whether it's for profit or not!

Judy

All told, we spent about six months getting the property into retreat-ready condition. But partway through that time, we paused for something special, something important.

We stopped our work in order to take time to thank the Lord, as a community, for what He had done for us.

In September of 2000, we had a dedication ceremony for Hilltop.

Gene

Many of the people in attendance were faculty from Talbot who had already visited the retreat center and so already had a familiarity with it and a fondness for it. But there were many other friends of the ministry—crowds of people—who streamed up the mountain in order to praise God in this new place that He'd set aside for His service.

Members of the board, faculty from Talbot, our own family and friends—they were all there.

JUDY

It was a day of rejoicing that we never forgot! The point of the whole day was to dedicate the property to God, for His service, and for the work that His Holy Spirit was going to do in the people that came up there to pray, and to rest, and to heal.

With all of the grunt work of the past few months behind us, it was time to celebrate God's faithfulness.

GENE

And we actually had an order of service all lined up for the celebration! We began the service mid-morning, at about 10:30 a.m. We set up folding chairs in the large meeting room at the top of the winding staircase. Because the carpet on the staircase was so well-cushioned, some people sat there instead of on the chairs! We had a podium set in front of the fireplace and flowers set along the hearth. The room was crowded—filled with people who had helped with the vision: friends, family, and colleagues.

It was an amazing day. When I think back to the list of people who were on the docket to pray and to speak and to sing at the dedication ceremony, I'm really humbled. These were great men: Ray Ortlund, the faithful pastor; Sam Metcalf, a minister to ministers; Dennis Dirks, the dean of Talbot School of Theology and a dedicated leader and teacher; Walt Harrah, the gifted and inspirational musician; Bruce Narramore, a clinical psychologist and founder of the Narramore Center; Bruce's wife, Kathy Narramore, a woman with a tender heart for missionaries; J.P. Moreland, a well-known philosopher who spoke and said of Hilltop, "This story needs to be told over and over; it is the story of God's miracles of today"; and Walt Russell, a thoughtful theologian and a dear friend, along with his wife, Marty.

It was a weighty moment to see them all assembled there on the mountain, ready to bless our new endeavor.

JUDY

And don't forget Gayle Zamora, who had sent me the verse from Habakkuk that held me in the vision when I was tempted to doubt! She also helped us decorate the house once it had been cleaned up. And Don Carr, Noah Mudderland, and Dave Rhode were there too - longtime friends of our son Gregg. Don, a chef in the making, who made sure that we all were well fed after the dedication ceremony leaving Noah and Dave to find parking for everyone. Truly, we were beyond blessed by the enormous amount of time and talent represented by the friends that gathered around us that day. Even given all the names Gene mentioned already, we're still leaving out so many important people—it would be impossible to list them all, but the presence of every one of them was a gift that I treasure to this day.

We were blessed by everyone who was willing to speak at the dedication, and then Gene and I were able to say a few words too.

As I stood there, looking out at this amazing group of people, and standing with my own two feet on the ground of the retreat center that had first come to me as a vision in the night, I was overwhelmed by the goodness of God and tears of joy flowed down my face.

And so that was what I shared with those who were gathered there. I recounted what I'd come to call our "stones of remembrance"—those moments and place-markers in the history of Hilltop that stood like altars made out of solid rock, reminders that called me to worship. Every time I'd wavered on this journey, God had done something else to remind me to hold fast, to remind me that He was still there, to remind me that He was the One guiding us and directing us.

I remembered sharing the vision with Gene. With our kids. With Walt and Sherry, and with so many others.

I remembered the pieces of scripture God had other people drop into my path, to hold me when I was doubting.

I remembered Walt Russell pointing at me, and telling me, "This one is still yours," before I'd ever told him about the vision God had sent me.

I remembered the miraculous year-to-date donation, and the even more miraculous half-million-dollar check.

I remembered all the people who'd given of their time, their expertise, their talent, in order to bring us to this place.

As we mentioned before, even as God continued to lead us, we often felt the way the Israelites must have felt as they wandered in the wilderness: lost and confused and alone. But the truth was that as God had never stopped being faithful to them, and He had never stopped being faithful to us.

He is always faithful to give to us out of His own goodness.

Truly, I felt like I could echo the words of Moses, and so that's what I did, closing my remarks on that glorious day with these verses from Deuteronomy 1:

> The LORD your God, who is going before you, will fight for you, as he did for you in Egypt, before your very eyes, and in the wilderness. There you saw how the LORD your God carried you, as a father carries his son, all the way you went until you reached this place. (Deuteronomy 1:30-31)

Original Hilltop sign

Original Hilltop property

Chapter Twelve

Fully Operational

Judy

It's hard to come down from a high like that September of 2000 dedication service—especially when you're still literally up on a mountain peak! But now that Hilltop was dedicated and functional, it was time to begin the real work of the ministry.

Gene

Yet even though Hilltop was technically functional, it was still very bare-bones. There was no real furniture or furnishings. The people coming up on retreat found themselves sitting on lawn chairs instead of couches and sleeping on camping mats instead of real beds.

Judy

Given that we were now deeply in debt, we had no idea where we would get the money to buy everything that this gigantic, four-story house needed.

Gene

To tell the truth, it was a kind of scary time in our lives, simply because the operation of Hilltop involved so much uncertainty. It was often hard to remember our primary purpose up there: to help people to spend time alone with the Lord, to help ministers be refreshed.

It was hard to remember because we ourselves were so buried in the minutiae. It was a constant running list in our heads: *We have to get the rooms ready, we have to get enough beds, we have to get this place usable, we have to keep the mortgage paid up.*

Even though we were there trying to provide a space where the busy details of daily life drop away—and we *did* manage to provide a space like that for others—we ourselves became, if possible, even more bound up in the small urgencies of daily life.

And the financial urgencies were certainly part of that. We were trying to make things go, but if the ministry didn't bring in enough in any given month, Judy and I had to make up the slack out of our own wallet.

That happened a lot, in the beginning.

Judy

It was overwhelming.

At the same time, it was exciting. Hilltop was actually in existence! It was actually being used!

It was actually being a blessing to people in the Kingdom of God.

In addition to some of the more prosaic things—like fixing the heating—we worked on things that made the house more beautiful and usable. Gayle Zamora was one friend who helped us transform ugliness into beauty without spending a lot of money. She had that gift. Gene's two brothers, Harley and Jerry, and their wives, came and helped to wallpaper and paint under Gayle's direction. We had so much fun making Hilltop inviting and hospitable! Gayle and I spent hundreds of hours looking for things to enhance Hilltop without spending a fortune. Eventually, we were also able to buy some pews from a church in Pasadena. We installed them on the top floor of the house, which instantly transformed that big upper room into a meditative space for prayer. We also found a print of Jesus praying in the Garden of Gethsemane to hang in the chapel space, and a five-foot painting of the Prodigal Son to hang in the entrance, along with a beautiful guestbook for people to sign. We felt this served as a symbol of Jesus welcoming those who entered the house.

By fall of the next year, we'd seen the center used by everyone from seminary students to individual pastors to the entire leadership staffs of various churches. Hundreds of people had come up to Hilltop, spent time in solitude with the Lord, and gone home changed.

I saved some of the comments people gave me back in those days. It just meant so much to be able to read and reread them. They said things like this:

"God has accomplished a great work in my heart and mind and given me new direction. The…surroundings fed my physical need and helped to soothe a troubled soul so that God could gently redirect me in a way that I should go."

"We praise God for this time of renewal and solitude. Our souls have been refreshed and our spirits feel cleansed. The beauty of Hilltop—both inside and out—the blessed silence, is unique in California. We have been renewed and better equipped to face ministry in the concrete, asphalt, and stucco down the mountain."

"My time with the Lord was water to my soul and I left the mountain feeling refreshed and renewed."

To receive feedback like that...well, let's just say: it made it all worth it.

Gene

Yet there were some things we still could not do—things we really wanted to get done! For instance, we really wanted to form an endowment for needy pastors. That was meant to be a fund that would basically provide scholarships for ministers who needed something like Hilltop, but who didn't have the money to pay the basic fee we requested (these fees weren't exorbitant; they were just to cover some of the basic operating expenses).

Judy

There were so many big dreams we had that were still in the ministry's future at that point. We had to take the first steps first—steps like getting furniture and dishes.

And there, yet once again, the Lord provided.

We were able to make contact with Gibson Glass, a company who agreed to sell us dishes and flatware below wholesale prices. This was an amazing gift and when we took them up on it, they took us to their warehouse and let us loose, telling us to pick out whatever we wanted.

We picked out enough dishes to serve 50 people at a time—including pots and pans and other accessories, like baking utensils. We were able to get all the dishes that the retreat center needed for about $1,500.

That was definitely a God thing.

Gene

That was one miracle from God. But the other was even more miraculous: the Campus Loft furniture company straight out *asked* us to give them our wish-list for furniture for Hilltop. They let us pick out anything we wanted. We'd managed to scrape together $10,000 for furnishings, and we went to them, hoping that with their generous willingness to help us out, $10,000 would be enough.

We were stunned when they allowed us to purchase everything we asked for—worth far more than the $10,000 we spent.

Their generosity—and God's generosity through them—was astonishing.

Judy

Just as God had provided the property, He provided the items to fill it.

It is things like that which make me say that Hilltop is living proof of Ephesians 3:20:

> Now glory be to God who by his mighty power at work within us is able to do far more than we would ever dare to ask or even dream of—infinitely beyond our highest prayers, desires, thoughts, or hopes. (TLB)

One business helped us to get dishes, and another helped us to get furniture, and the inside of that four-story, 8,000-square-foot house began to have a beautiful interior that matched the beauty of the lovely grounds that surrounded it.

We could never have achieved any of this without Him. It was His blessing and kindness that made everything happen, and it's our desire that, from beginning to end, from visionary ideas to small details, Hilltop will be a testament to God's power. It's His handiwork, spawned by His goodness, molded by His will.

We wanted to testify this truth to everyone who came to Hilltop, and one way we were able to do that was through the gift of an artist I met through one of my speaking engagements. I was speaking at a local church when a woman came up to me afterwards with her daughter, and volunteered to paint a mural on the wall of Hilltop—a mural that would illustrate the miracles that God had performed to bring Hilltop into existence. She painted a river-rock pathway on the wall of the main meeting room, and when you stepped back, you saw that embedded in the rock path was the word *VISION*. On each rock we were to write the miracles God did as a testimony to the fact that God provided this place for those who came to give Him glory. It was such a beautiful mural, and so wonderful that God gave her this artistic gift that she then shared with us!

I am so excited—still, to this day—by the gift that God has given us in providing for this ministry, and I spend my days continually watching and waiting to see what He will do next.

I feel blessed just to be a part of His divine plan.

Gene

And we were certainly a big part of the plan! Even as the property became more trim, neat, and lovely, Judy and I found ourselves becoming more exhausted, stretched thin, and worn down.

From Monday morning till Friday afternoon, I would work long hours at my corporate job and Judy would work long hours at the university.

Then, from Friday afternoon until Sunday night, we would be up at Hilltop, prepping the retreats, sometimes leading the retreats, cooking the meals, and then cleaning up once everyone left.

We'd vacuum every one of those 8,000 square feet (that alone took four hours!) and make every one of those 30 beds.

Judy

And clean every one of those five bathrooms—you can't leave them out!

GENE

Then we'd drive back down the mountain and start it all over again.

We did that for three years straight.

JUDY

There was some variation in there—don't get us wrong! Some dear friends, Joy and Shawn Hofer, had a heart for the ministry at Hilltop and they helped out in those early years. Some of those meals for multitudes were prepared by them. Also, we briefly had a part-time employee that helped out, but our budget couldn't really bear the weight of that employee, and so that didn't last long, even though we needed the help.

But God did give us people who were excited about what was going on up there, who were able to help us, and that was an amazing blessing.

One of those people was Paul Jensen. He led retreats up at Hilltop even before I did! In some ways, I interned under him, watching how he did things, and learning as we went along.

Paul was an adjunct faculty member at Talbot and also had his own nonprofit organization, The Leadership Institute, which took pastors through a two-year program of deepening their relationships with God through solitude, silence, and retreat. As I, along with other faculty, was developing the ICD (Intentional Character Development) program at Talbot, Paul offered to lead some of our early retreats, which helped set the tone and tenor for future retreats. I participated as he mentored me in how to facilitate a retreat where hearts were prepared and open to the Holy Spirit's work in them. Later, wanting more of the faculty to be able to mentor and invest in students, the faculty of Talbot was also asked to lead and facilitate the student groups they brought up on retreat.

In some of those early days, I really began to see how the Holy Spirit could use the sharing of our stories in order to bring people more deeply into relationship with Him. And God doesn't use just the leader of the retreat to speak into peoples' lives—He uses everyone there, the whole community!

Because of what we learned in those early days of leading retreats, the sharing of stories became an important part of what Hilltop continued to do. I still, to this day, want to do more of that—especially with pastors and their spouses. When you can get couples in ministry up there together with others like them—especially when those other couples aren't a part of their own denomination, so there isn't the pressure of *performing* for the people you work with day in and day out—a lot of growth can happen. It's good to get people out of their power structures and into a different, freer kind of community, at least occasionally.

When you see how God is working in the lives of others, it helps you to see how He is working in your own life, and the life of your family and friends.

Gene

We had huge retreats in those days. We'd take a bunch of students, everyone who was in that particular class at Talbot, and take them all up to Hilltop. We got more personal over the years—started working with smaller groups—but back then it was bigger retreats, which took a lot of work.

JUDY

At the end of Sunday nights, before we went back down the mountain, we'd grab dinner at a little Victorian house converted into a restaurant in Cedar Pines Park. They made wonderful home-cooked meals. We'd feel our bodies and hearts rest in the truth of what was happening. We'd pause and reflect, and we'd say, "This is amazing."

We actually sat there and noticed that it had happened. It *was* happening. God had actually provided this—all this. We were actually doing it.

That was kind of surreal at first: that we were *actually doing it.*

GENE

It's still surreal. I walk up there and think, *This is unbelievable.*

JUDY

It's way beyond anything we could have imagined. That house was so beautiful...so comfortable!

GENE

Yes, and, looking back, I think we were too invested in making it comfortable—at least, we focused more on that than maybe we should have. It was important—I still believe that—but it wasn't the *most* important thing.

Judy

We were thinking more about the physical care of the buildings in those days, and less about spiritual formation. Honestly, I think that was because we just didn't know enough about it yet, despite all my work in the subject both in my PhD program at Fuller and in beginning the program at Talbot!

But it was the beginning of things, so it makes sense we experienced a fair amount of trial and error.

Gene

Some things you only learn by doing. One of the things that we eventually changed was how strict we were about who could use the property. At that point, we needed money in order to keep everything going and so if, say, the Chamber of Commerce wanted to come up and hold a more corporate-type retreat, we let them.

We just needed to keep the thing occupied.

That changed, after what happened in the fall of 2003.

Judy

Everything changed in 2003. But this was a year or two before that, and we had no idea what was coming. All we knew was that the ministry was flourishing, and we were delighted, busy, and completely overwhelmed—though not always in that order!

Even though we sometimes let secular groups use the property, it really was largely being used by ministers, missionaries, church staff, and seminary students. We were able to watch, week after week, as the Lord used Hilltop in their lives.

It was a sort of dual journey: watching what was happening in the retreatants' lives, and watching what was happening in our own lives. There was some mirroring there. Some of the broken relationships they suffered from made us conscious of the stresses in our own lives—stress connected to identity, money, and career. Gene, for instance, was still in the rat-race of corporate America, but he couldn't spend weekend after weekend up at Hilltop, in this beautiful, holy atmosphere without beginning to change.

Without a growing desire for something different.

Gene

That's putting it poetically. The truth was that I was spending most of my weekends as a jack-of-all-trades up at Hilltop—serving in whatever capacity needed. Much of what was needed was hard physical labor, and it was getting wearing to do that every weekend and then to return to a full week of corporate work.

So it's true that by the summer of 2001, I was beginning to think seriously about what I wanted to do for the rest of my life—to the point that I asked our Board of Directors to begin praying for me as I tried to discern the direction in which the Lord wanted me to go. I knew I needed guidance as we continued to develop the ministry at Hilltop.

I'd been in corporate business all of my life, though. Even considering doing something different was a huge step for me.

JUDY

Despite Gene's slowly growing feeling that he needed to make a change, his corporate experience continued to be a huge blessing for Hilltop. Running the ministry at Hilltop wasn't just continual car trips and housework, it also involved board meetings, communication with sponsors, and forward-thinking planning and development.

Gene excelled at all of that.

GENE

I did do a lot of work keeping our donors in the loop and looking ahead at what Hilltop might grow to be in the future.

For instance, I worked to build a relationship with an architect who might be able to help us develop the land further. We got aerial photos and a survey of the property made in order to aid in that effort.

Working alongside the architect, who was from a group called HMC, we aimed to put together a master plan for future buildings on the site. The goal was to be able to accommodate more people. We wanted to build some outlying housing for missionaries on furlough, and we also hoped to have a chapel with a prayer walk, as well as single units to provide spaces for people on individual retreats.

JUDY

Hilltop belonged to God and it was truly His project, but we couldn't help but have our own dreams and desires for the future of the ministry. We were beginning to have to turn people away, simply because we didn't have the facilities their particular group needed. We wanted to change that.

We saw how Hilltop was providing refreshment for thirsty souls, and we simply wanted that ministry to increase.

GENE

We had big dreams and yet…we had dwindling personal resources. Up the mountain, down the mountain. Work down in the valley, work up in the heights.

We were working three jobs at once. It was a lot. Something had to give.

JUDY

The truth is that we were doing the very thing to ourselves that we were asking people to come up to Hilltop to have *not happen to them.* That rest and refreshment that Hilltop offered? It was the one thing our lives were truly missing.

How could we ask pastors to find a rest that we ourselves were neglecting?

GENE

I remember telling Judy, "Something's got to give. We can't keep this up."

JUDY

We didn't know what the solution was, but we both saw the problem.

How could we ask pastors to come up to a renewal center to learn to rest in the presence of the Lord, when we ourselves were running from rest as fast as we possibly could?

Gene was right: something was going to have to give. But what?

Attendees on stairwell during dedication

Gene and Judy speaking during dedication

Chapter Thirteen

Total Dedication

Judy

By 2003, we'd known for a while that something was going to have to change: we could not keep living the way we were living. Every week we worked hard at our regular jobs down in the valley. And every weekend, we went up to Hilltop and worked hard at our ministry up on the mountain.

Up and down. Down and up. No rest, no stopping.

Something had to change, and we both could see that clearly. But the solution remained elusive for many long months.

As we talked about the situation we were in, there was one step that seemed to present itself more and more clearly as the solution: one of us should quit working our regular job. But which one?

To my astonishment, Gene was determined that he should be the one to do it.

Gene

I didn't think it was astonishing at all; I thought it was a no-brainer!

After all, it was Judy's connections at Talbot that were the most useful in guiding pastors, seminarians, and other ministers towards Hilltop. She should be the one to keep working at her job, because her job was so closely related to our ministry.

I prayed about it for well over a year, and asked other trusted folks—including our directors—to pray with me. It got to the point where it was just crystal-clear in my mind: I needed to quit my job and dedicate myself to full-time ministry.

But Judy was hesitant to have us take that step.

Judy

Is it any surprise that I was hesitant? Gene had been in corporate America for our entire marriage! It had been *decades* since we'd known any other kind of life. Our marriage was well-worn-in, but it was also vibrant and comforting and deeply loving. Changing the status quo meant changing something that was already going really well. I didn't know what our lives would look like if Gene made this change; all I knew is that we'd be moving into a marital future unlike any we'd ever known so far.

The unknown is always a bit intimidating, even when you're stepping into it for healthy, wise reasons.

Gene

It was a strange kind of role reversal: at the beginning of our Hilltop journey, when God gave Judy the vision, I was the one who hesitated over practical questions. I was the one asking, *Where's the money going to come from? How is this going to change our lives?*

Now it was Judy asking those kinds of questions.

Judy

To be fair, those kinds of questions needed answers! We live in one of the most expensive places in the country, and the way we handled that was by being a two-income family. How were we going to live on just my income when our budget was built around both of us working—and especially around Gene's success in the corporate world?

I trusted Gene though, and if this was the step he wanted to take, I was bound and determined to back him up. So I started doing feverish calculations. Could I take on more classes, more clients?

But then Gene said something that both rocked me back on my heels *and* made me instantly calmer. He said, "No, honey. This is going to be my responsibility, not yours. You don't have to take on any more work. Not one more client. Not one more class. *I don't want you doing any more than you're already doing.*"

It was so kind. But I had to ask… "Then how are we going to make it work?"

"Honey," said Gene, "don't you know that if we can't make it, I'll just go back out and get another job? I'm not asking you to carry my weight. Just do what you're doing, and don't do one bit more."

Those words put my fears to rest.

Gene

I did not want Judy taking on additional work because of my decision—and she didn't—but there were a few sacrifices we both had to make, the biggest of which was selling our large family house, and buying and moving into a smaller one.

Our kids were grown and gone, and so it made sense in other ways too, but it certainly was a change, and we couldn't *not* notice it.

Judy

I admit, I had a hard time giving up our family home. I thought we would never find a smaller home I would like and feel comfortable in—and we didn't! The home we found was in a quiet neighborhood backing up to the foothills and it was priced at what we could afford on my Talbot income. All of that was good! But...I didn't like the house. It just didn't have that feel that I love in a home.

I learned, again, like I had at the Hilltop house, that I needed help in order to see the potential. My friend Leah Hutchinson, an interior decorator, came over and gave me the gift of sight that I needed. After a summer of work redecorating, tearing down old walls, and putting up new ones, that smaller house became the house I was hoping for!

Again, God knew what I needed long before I did.

Gene

I also had to take the time to prepare a good and thoughtful exit from my work; I appreciated my colleagues in the corporate world and I didn't want to leave any of them in the lurch.

But I did that preparation with a feeling of freedom. I was making this change because *I* had changed. I wasn't the same man I'd been for the past few decades. It's hard for me to put my finger on exactly when things had turned around for me, but I'd come to a place where I was able to stop chasing the next paycheck, the next deal, the next bonus.

If you want to look at it from a practical, earthly perspective, I can point to a few tangible things: I'd been investing long enough that I knew we had a cushion, I had enough experience to know I could find work again if I needed to. That stuff was there, and I won't deny that it was reassuring to me.

But it was still a brand-new sort of life I was stepping into and if you want to look at it from a spiritual perspective, I guess all I can say is that it was a God-thing. Bottom line: it was that God brought me to the place where I was able to give it all up.

He brought me to the place where I was able to walk away.

JUDY

Gene is down-playing it a bit, I think. From his perspective, it all made sense, it all followed. The logic of heaven and the logic of earth are all, well, *logical* to him.

But to me, it was like a whirlwind had picked us up, spun us around, and deposited us on an entirely new planet!

To turn Gene from someone who was so money-motivated into someone who was not going to take *one cent* for his work? That was a complete turnaround. That was something only the Lord could have done.

Gene had been totally focused on climbing the ladder—and he'd been successful at it too! So many people only dream of getting to the top; Gene had actually done it.

For a man like that—driven, successful—to be able to leave the rat race that so many Americans are so obsessed with? It was a huge step of faith.

For a man who had defined himself by his ability to generate a good income to move into completely charitable volunteer work? That's a miracle.

When Gene decided to dedicate himself completely to ministry, he determined that he was not going to profit off the ministry at all. He was not going to take a paycheck. He was not going to be remunerated.

And you know what? He's kept that promise. Since he dedicated himself completely to Hilltop, he hasn't made one cent off the ministry.

All of the work he does now is work for the Lord, not for himself.

That kind of change is miraculous.

That's the kind of change that only God can do.

Gene

Well, I'm certainly willing to give God the credit, because from my point of view, I was only doing what was most reasonable! So if there's any big miracle there, it certainly wasn't from me.

Once I'd decided to quit my job, we started doing all the practical work of downsizing. Like I said: we sold our house and moved into a smaller one. I wrapped up my projects at my job.

We got all of the loose ends tied up by the end of the summer of 2003, right before my 60th birthday.

Judy

Gene's 60th birthday turned out to be such a joyous occasion! Of course milestone birthdays are often fun to celebrate, but this day was something more. On Gene's birthday, he officially dedicated himself to full-time ministry. We held a big party, and many friends came over, including friends from Talbot and from Hilltop's board, like Dennis Dirks and Sam Metcalf.

At the party, these men of faith laid their hands on Gene and prayed for him and commissioned him into full-time ministry. It was a beautiful, wonderful day—a day when we knew we were finally fully committed to doing this thing that God had asked us to do, and we were committed to doing it *together.*

We were so encouraged by the people who had come alongside us and empowered Gene to take up this new vocation. We walked away from his birthday thinking that this new stage of our life was going to last for years.

We had no idea what was coming.

Gene

We had no idea what was coming, but we were totally caught up in what was going on in the moment. And that was a good thing.

There was so much to do at Hilltop and by quitting my corporate job, I finally *actually had the time to get it done.*

I can't even begin to express what an exhilarating change that was.

Before, it felt like we were constantly treading water, but never getting anywhere.

Now, we were putting in just as much work, but all that effort was actually pushing us forward. We swam against the current, but, stroke after stroke, we were actually moving towards that finish line. We could *see* the progress we were making.

Judy

That's true! It was amazing how much Gene was able to get done just in the few short months after his commissioning!

Gene's full-time attention made the ministry flourish. Everything was getting done—faster and more thoroughly than ever before. Projects that had been dawdling along, getting worked on a bit at a time, Gene could now tackle and complete lickety-split.

Those were halcyon days. The world felt wide open to us.

It was such a change for me, too. I know Gene's talked about how God brought him to the place where he felt he could step down from his work, but that had been a hard transition for me. It took me a long time to get used to the idea that we were going to live on one salary, because we'd always depended so much on Gene's income.

God had asked us to step out in faith. I had to trust that *He* was going to take care of us, that *He* was going to make this happen.

That it wasn't going to be something that came from us.

After all, because of Gene's work, we'd become really used to all the comforts of life. We lived well. We took beautiful vacations. I remember getting to go to places like Monaco, overlooking the Mediterranean, because Gene was given the trip as a reward for being sales manager of the year.

It was one of the loveliest places in the whole wide world, and I had to look at that memory and think, *Am I willing to give this up? What if we never travel again? What if I never see the beauty of other places in the world? Will we still have comforts? Will we struggle horribly?*

The truth was that I didn't want to quit traveling. Corporate life had allowed us to go places we never could have gone to otherwise—Gene had, through his work, won trips to Europe and Hawaii. It was luxurious and wonderful and I didn't want to give it up! My income had already become smaller when I gave up my counseling practice in order to focus on spiritual formation work at Talbot and I couldn't imagine how we'd ever have enough to travel to fun places again.

(Looking back now, the amazing thing is that we've traveled more since Gene stepped down from corporate life than we ever did before! God knew that was a desire of my heart and He is so kind. He is a loving, gracious God who has brought my work to places I never would have dreamed of visiting! But I had no idea of that future back then. No idea at all.)

Working through those doubts made me realize that, in many ways, my security was more in who Gene was and what he provided than in who *God* was and what *He* provided. That was a humbling realization.

But God is so kind. He helped me to see who He was, and what He could do—and one of the main ways He showed me that was through Hilltop. Hilltop brought all those separate threads of our lives together—our fears and our doubts, sure, but also our faith and our potential for ministry.

Through Hilltop, God helped us to let go of the things we trusted in that weren't secure (but that we *thought* were secure). He helped us to let go of those worldly things and to actually trust in Him—in the God who provided it all in the first place, and who could continue to provide exactly what we needed for fulfillment and for happiness.

Most of all, God provided us with love. In our ministry at Hilltop, we discovered an even deeper love for God and for one another, because by walking into the vision together, we learned to wait, to pray, to listen, and to ask questions. We learned intimacy with God by giving up the things we *thought* held the keys to our happiness, and instead we grasped hold of a greater happiness—a happiness and joy that only God can give.

Hilltop was our salvation in many ways. It was a salvation of finding intimacy with God and with one another. That kind of intimacy brings the joy that John 15 talks about. "You make my joy complete." Those were words we could say and mean now.

We understood those words of Jesus at a whole deeper level.

And that's what Hilltop was really all about.

Gene

It's funny how the spiritual and the tangible are so intertwined in this life. Hilltop was absolutely about all the things Judy just laid out.

It was also absolutely about the physical retreat house: about the walls and the floors and the literal, tangible space that God provided for people to work out these spiritual truths.

I loved that I got to do such hands-on, practical work for the Kingdom of Heaven.

And there was a lot to do! At that point in the life of the ministry, there was a lot going on. In addition to finishing up the repairs and refurbishment of the house itself, we were working on things like bringing in more ministry partners, doing the groundwork for eventual expansion, and bringing in the funds needed to retire the mortgage. We also found a large fifth-wheel trailer that we put on the property. This gave Judy and I a place to relax outside of the retreat house itself. It was important to us not to have any of our personal belongings in Hilltop—we wanted it to be clear to people who came up on retreat that they were in God's house, not ours. We didn't want to live in the retreat house; we wanted it to stay a dedicated place for the people who had come up to find a deeper intimacy with God.

We didn't want to expand the physical footprint of Hilltop until we were entirely debt-free, so paying off the mortgage was a huge priority. Still, while I worked on that part of the problem, I also started laying the groundwork for the future.

That was the big picture. In the week-to-week life of Hilltop, we were still holding regular retreats for Christians in ministry and students from Talbot who needed time alone with God. That part of the ministry was so rewarding, because at this point, we had gotten really good at doing the very kind of work that Hilltop was meant to do: people were coming up to the mountain, spending intimate time with the Lord, and going home refreshed, renewed, and changed.

The Hilltop house was beautiful. It was now completely furnished—no more beach chairs and camping mattresses! The upper room now served as a chapel, complete with a communion table, and it had a breathtaking view of Lake Silverwood and the beautiful trees and skyline.

We were working on a partnership with the Institute for Spiritual Formation at Biola and we were also applying for a grant that would provide a two-year program of spiritual direction for inner-city pastors.

There were a lot of projects being juggled and a lot of excitement in the air.

JUDY

What we were providing at Hilltop was so important. As one of our brochures at the time pointed out, to schedule planned times of withdrawal from the busyness of a life of ministry for solitude and spiritual disciplines was to follow the pattern of our Lord. Jesus often withdrew to pray and He taught His disciples to do likewise.

Jesus knew His Father was with Him in ministry, but He also knew that He had to find time to be still and silent in the presence of His Father, to be empowered by His Father and loved by Him. He could then return to the burdens of ministry filled with an experience of the Father's loving and faithful presence. Jesus made a regular habit of spending time alone in prayer, and those intentional times of devotion renewed His strength for continued ministry.

If Jesus needed those times alone in prayer, and He is the Son of God and God Himself, how could we possibly need less? It's important for us to follow the pattern set by our Lord during His time here on Earth.

GENE

Hilltop was not unique in that it offered a place for retreat, but it did have four unique qualities that set it apart from other retreat centers:

1) Its tie-in with a seminary.

2) Its location. (It was right outside a major city; you didn't have to drive hours to get there, as you did with many other retreat centers.) It was also in a beautiful place surrounded by God's created beauty which drew you to Him.

3) It offered *preventative* care. (It wasn't a crisis center; it was a place that prevented crises from happening in the first place. It also was not an entertainment center—this was a place for retreats. It was not a summer camp.)

4) It was Protestant. (There were Catholic retreat centers that were similar to Hilltop, but there was a dearth of Protestant ones, and we needed them.)

In the fall of 2003, we could confidently say that Hilltop was finally the place that Judy had seen in her vision. It was finally operating the way we'd dreamed it would.

There was ongoing work to do, of course, and there were changes now and again. One of the hardest came when Ray Ortlund died, which was a great sorrow. We missed him sorely. Our son, Gregg, kindly volunteered to fill the gap left in our Board of Directors and was waiting on approval from the rest of the board.

The vision had become a reality.

Three months after my 60th birthday and my commissioning to full-time ministry, I finished painting the *very last room* in that gigantic, 8,000-square-foot house.

The very last room.

Hilltop wasn't just a reality; it was complete.

And then came the fire.

Chapter Fourteen

Is This a Cruel Joke?

Judy

Gene was now completely dedicated to Hilltop, but my work as a professor continued, and in the course of that work, I was invited to travel to Boston to speak at the North American Professors of Christian Education (NAPCE) conference. Gene planned to travel with me.

Even though we were going to be on the other side of the country, there was still a retreat happening at Hilltop. It was a local church group we were very familiar with, and so we were able to trust them with the clean-up and lock-up, and the other work of running the retreat center for the week. In circumstances like that, Gene has guidelines set up for them to follow and is always available by cell phone if they have questions or need anything.

The NAPCE conference was in October, and we expected to meet with cool, pleasant weather out in Massachusetts—

which would be very different than what we were leaving behind in Southern California!

The joke we tell out in Los Angeles is that we don't have four seasons, we only have two: the rainy season and the dry season. In good years, L.A. gets a nice, soaking amount of rain during the early part of the year—about January to March. And that has to be enough to keep us going until the calendar pages flip over to January once again. After early spring, it's pretty much sunny days for the rest of the year. You can see why desert-adapted plants are what really thrive out where we are!

But 2003 found California in drought conditions. There hadn't been that much rain in the winter, and by the time we'd made our way through the long, hot, scorching days of summer, the soil was cracked and dry, the foliage was crisp and brown, and the land was parched—even up in the San Bernardino mountains. All those tall, rangy pine trees were just full of combustible sap...and they would go up like torches with only one single spark.

Gene

Of course, the possibility of fire wasn't on our minds at all as we traveled out to Boston! Our minds were on the trip, on Judy's upcoming presentation, on the people we would see. It was only three months since I'd quit my job to dedicate myself to full-time ministry. We were actually feeling really good as we headed out on this trip. I'd been able to accomplish so much in the ministry just in the short time since I'd completely committed to it—as I said, right before we left, I'd actually put the finishing touches of paint on the very last room in that gigantic, 8,000-square foot house. I'd walked away from my birthday, from that day of dedication, feeling very encouraged by the people who had been there and prayed for me. I was thinking that this new phase of my life was going to last for years.

We knew the group we'd left behind at the house, we were happy with the work that was being done on a weekly and monthly basis, and we were excited about the short break—even though this was, of course, a working trip for Judy.

Judy

I was scheduled to speak on Tuesday or Wednesday, so I spent the beginning of the conference week reconnecting with colleagues, attending the other lectures—that sort of thing. But on Monday…on Monday we saw that Arrowhead was in the news.

And it was in the news because it was on fire.

Gene

Not the town itself, but very close by, in the forest. There were evacuations, there was a huge fire-fighting effort—but this whole section of the mountainside was on fire. It was a big deal, a very big deal. Big enough that it made the news even out there in Boston.

JUDY

So, at first, we were just keeping our eyes on the news.

I mean...Hilltop was very close to Arrowhead, so we knew that anything like this that threatened Arrowhead was also a threat to us.

GENE

When we first heard, I didn't think too much of it. I thought, *There's no way Hilltop's going to burn; we're fine.*

I did keep watching the news though, any chance I could get.

JUDY

I didn't feel quite as sanguine as Gene did, but there wasn't anything we could do about it from where we were, and I had work to do there at the conference, so we just watched.

And prayed.

GENE

And then we got a phone call.

The group up at Hilltop had been evacuated. That's when we knew, for sure, that the fire really was a threat not just to Arrowhead—but to Hilltop.

JUDY

Watching and waiting was all we could do while we were at the conference, but as soon as we got back home, our first thought was, *How fast can we get up that mountain?*

Unfortunately, we found out, that was no longer an option. The fire had grown too big, and had come much, much too close.

Gene

We weren't allowed up. No one was. They had closed the whole mountain to everyone except emergency personnel and maybe some news crews. So it was back to watching the news, hoping, somehow, that the shots from the helicopters would include some bit of land that we recognized. And they did—once. There was one shot I saw that included the house at Hilltop. That let me know it was still standing. It was this brief glimpse of hope.

But that hope was quickly extinguished.

Judy

From our new, smaller home down in the valley, in a Los Angeles suburb called Brea, we continued watching and waiting. The news reports came every hour of the day. The fires were being fought by expert firefighters. The fires were being held back...no, the fires were still growing.

The uncertainty was agony, but then the uncertainty ended—and the reality was even worse.

Gene

Three days after returning home, one of our neighbors from up in the mountains called us, at about 3:00 p.m. He said that he'd taken his dirt bike and gone up to see what was going on, using the back roads to make his way around the travel restrictions. He'd wanted to see if his house was burning or not.

He was the one who broke to us the staggering truth.

He said, "Hilltop is gone."

Judy

It was such a shock. I asked him, "How do you know?"

He said, "I'm standing on the driveway and the flames are going over my head."

I found out later that it was actually more like the property was smoldering at that point, but he said, "the flames," and that image has never left my memory since.

His house, by the way, ended up surviving. It was on a different part of the slope than Hilltop. There was a road about a quarter mile from the Hilltop house where they took down a bunch of trees to stop the fire from going further. So all of our neighbors to the back of us didn't get burned down, but the houses of our neighbors alongside of us on the ridge were all destroyed.

Gene

Near Hilltop, the fire was so fierce. The firemen had ended up building a backfire to stave the fire off, but then the winds switched direction, and the backfire raced around Lake Silverwood (out of which the helicopters were scooping water to drop on the fire) and then went roaring straight up the mountain. Hilltop sat kind of on the edge of the mountain, and so it was the first one to get hit.

There was a fire hydrant right in front of Hilltop, so the firemen attached their hoses and were spraying there.

The house was built of good materials, so it didn't just start burning. But then the fire got in under the rafters, under the eaves. The firemen said that, after that, the house basically just imploded.

The fire got so raging hot that they literally had to flee. Their hoses were still lying on the driveway; conditions changed so fast that they had to abandon them. They ran for their lives from the sheer heat of those walls of flame.

Judy

I remember our neighbor saying, "They did everything they could," and I really believe that they did. It was just too overwhelming. It was a natural disaster that no human power could have stopped—not quickly enough to save Hilltop.

"They did everything they could," he said, but the truth was that everything was gone.

My heart hurt, hearing that it was all gone. I prayed, *God, this isn't what we signed up for.*

We had waited so long, we had worked so hard, and now it was all dust and, quite literally, *ashes.*

Gene

When she says that everything was gone, she means it. It seems small alongside of the loss of the Hilltop house, but

Judy and I lost personal property too.

You see, we'd always wanted a clear line between our personal belongings and the ministry property. We didn't want people coming up on retreat to think that they were coming to *our* house. It was God's house. As we mentioned before, we never stayed in the Hilltop house itself. Instead, we parked a fifth-wheel trailer on the property—a trailer that belonged to us—and we stayed in that when we were up there working. We didn't want ministers on retreat to look around the house and think, "Oh, that must be Judy and Gene's, that must belong to their family." No. We wanted even the decorations in the house to point people towards God. Not us, never us.

JUDY

The decorations! Oh, that still makes me sad. The things we lost in the fire! The group that was up there that week—the ones who got evacuated—they didn't bring anything down out of the property, and how I wish they would have! There were such beautiful things that were lost, like these five-foot paintings we had up on Hilltop's walls, of Jesus in the Garden of Gethsemane and of the Prodigal Son. Our fifth-wheel could have been pulled off of the property too…

GENE

Yes, I wish they would have called us before they left. I mean, they had about twelve vehicles up there amongst them; a lot could have been fit in those. I would have said, "Well, if you're being evacuated, grab this, grab that!"

JUDY

It wasn't really their fault, though; I mean, we have the benefit of hindsight. They're such good people and they were being so conscientious—what they *did* do before they left was that they cleaned up. They made all the beds, they washed all the sheets, bless them! Adrenaline does such strange things to your thinking, and you really can't second-guess people who were on the ground, making the decisions in the face of all of that pressure and fear. They did the things that came automatically—I think we all act like that, in emergencies.

But there were losses that hurt, beyond just the loss of the house. We had a boat up there. I had grown up on a lake and boating was one way our family enjoyed vacationing. We'd owned a boat ever since we were married. Now that the kids were grown and gone, we had bought a new boat. Sometimes we'd take the students that came up down to Lake Silverwood to go water-skiing, during the longer retreats—the ones that lasted several weeks. The week before the fire, we'd pulled the boat out of Lake Silverwood, where we kept it on a slip, and took it up to Hilltop for the weekend. It was gone now, completely burned. And everything we'd kept in the fifth-wheel—like our cold-weather clothes, for when we were working up there in the winter—was gone, too. It was just a lot to take in.

GENE

You keep going after a disaster like that, though. That's the weird thing about life: something horrible happens, your whole world is changed, but does your whole world stop? No. You just keep going.

JUDY

So, one of the things we did was that we went to church. Of course. We're Christians. That's what we do. It's funny, because we'd actually *just* started attending a new church: North Hills Community Church in Brea. It was near our new home. We'd only been there one Sunday so far: the Sunday before the NAPCE conference out in Boston. We'd attended, we'd met the pastor and chatted with him, and let him know a little bit about ourselves and our work, but that was it. That was our only interaction with the folks there, so far.

GENE

On Wednesday we found out that Hilltop had burned to the ground and on Sunday we went to church at North Hills, where a man named Doug Green was the pastor. The fires were still going on. Doug Green talked about that during the service. He said, "You've seen the fires burning up in the mountains, and that doesn't really affect us—except that it actually does! Because we have a couple here in the church who had a retreat center up there that burned to the ground. Let's everyone gather around and pray for them."

We were brand new! It was only the second time we'd come there! And yet here this pastor was, stopping the whole service just to pray for us.

JUDY

That's when I really wept. That's when I felt it. That's the first time I really felt, "It's gone," not just with my mind, but with my heart.

There in that new church, surrounded by the people of God.

That's where it really hit me.

GENE

Doug had said that the fires didn't really affect them, but there actually was another ministry in the mountains they'd been praying for: Pinecrest Christian Camp, a camp up there that belonged to the Assemblies of God, their denomination.

We, as Hilltop, had actually had a deal with Pinecrest camp: that they'd send their small groups up to us, and any retreat groups we got that were too big for our facilities, we'd send down to them. So we did know the Pinecrest folks.

It was funny, because that connection ended up being really helpful in finally getting us up the mountain to see what had happened with our own eyes.

JUDY

Yes, because of Pine Crest's position and size, when we told the North Hills folks that we wanted to get up to Hilltop to see if there was anything we could do or save, they provided a way for us to get up there the next day, before the mountain was opened up to the general public. They worked out a special deal and got us up there.

Again, such an answer to prayer. Even in our sorrow, God was still there with us, going before us and providing for us.

Gene

So, on Monday, we headed up the mountain as a small group: us, our son Gregg and our son-in-law Jerry, and a few other good friends.

What we found once we got up was devastating.

Judy

It really was gone.

The ground was pocked and covered with ash. Everything was gray and desolate. It looked like nothing so much as the surface of the moon, dead and bare.

The house was gone; only the steel shaft of the elevator still stood, twisted and looming, like a broken skeleton, over what had once been a place full of prayer and laughter and peace.

Gene

This is what I had given my life to. This is what I had given up everything for. This...*nothing.*

I couldn't help but wonder what God was thinking.

I couldn't help but wonder if this whole thing, from the vision forward, was nothing but one long, cruel joke.

The 2003 fire on a hillside near Hilltop

Chapter Fifteen

What Was Left After the Fire

Judy

There we were, standing on the Hilltop property, looking at the ruins of that beautiful house. It was still smoldering. Small clouds of smoke drifted up from the wreckage, now and again.

I stood there, looking at it, and I couldn't even cry. I was so detached from my emotions, from what was going on.

I was looking at the devastation of all our hopes and my eyes were dry.

I just felt numb.

Gene

We could really see what we'd lost, once we were up there. And yet, at the same time, it wasn't something *we* had lost. Because it had never really been *ours* to begin with.

JUDY

It was a very strange moment. Hilltop was gone—clearly, literally, tangibly *gone*. And yet in our hearts, for some reason, we never thought the ministry was gone.

It just wasn't.

It was strange how, in the middle of that numbness, that fact could be so clear to us.

But it was perfectly clear: Hilltop, the house, was gone.

But the ministry was not.

The ministry was God's, and it wouldn't be gone until *He* said it was gone.

GENE

It's funny, because Judy got to say almost that exact thing—not just to the small group of us friends who'd traveled up there together—but to the whole world!

Coming right up behind us, as the roads began to be reopened to the evacuees, were the local news vans. Some of the crews followed us up to Hilltop—I guess because pictures are always more interesting with people in them, and there weren't many people allowed up there yet, so they had to make do with us.

So, there was that news crew, hoping to grab some good footage for their reports. And as we slowly wandered through the ruins left by the fire, a reporter came up to Judy, stuck a mic in her face, and asked her, "What will you do?"

And Judy said, "We trust that God will show us the next steps."

Judy

It wasn't until the words came out of my mouth that I realized that was exactly what I believed! As I said it, I realized I meant it: God would show us the next steps.

And we would follow Him.

Gene

It was honestly pretty cool to have Judy's declaration of faith broadcast out loud on the news. They asked her how she felt, asked her if we were going to rebuild. And she just replied that we'd do whatever God told us to do. And that was true.

The ministry we had labored on for years was now a barren wilderness, but neither of us felt that we were free to give it up. The ministry just didn't seem gone. Devastated, yes. Changed forever, yes. Mystifyingly tragic, yes.

Gone?

No.

Judy

We never thought it was over, but we did wonder, "What next?"

Being up there was hard. The air was still really smoky, and everywhere we walked there were memories. For instance, there was this great big granite rock next to the house—a huge boulder—and our son's sister-in-law had actually gotten married under an oak tree growing on the dirt embedded on the top of this rock. On that day after the fire, Gregg and I stood there for a while, just looking at that rock. The heat of the fire had actually peeled the granite off in layers. It seemed unbelievable that this place, once so full of such joy, was now so empty.

We went back down the mountain. Life went on. I taught my classes at Biola, Gene communicated with the Board about next steps.

And we waited to see what God would tell us to do.

Gene

The folks at Biola were actually a real high point in the midst of all that bleakness. *The Chimes*, the student newspaper, interviewed us and others who'd been up to Hilltop and did a whole write-up about the fire. Students who'd been up for our programs said very kind things about how Hilltop had helped them learn to be quiet in the presence of the Lord, helped them find peace and tranquility, and had helped them find a deeper love for God and an experience of His love for them. They commented on what a loss this was for the entire community there at Biola.

We started getting donations coming into the nonprofit, from people who hoped we would rebuild.

And then Talbot did a chapel focused on the ministry. That was very truly special because they grieved the loss with us.

Judy

It was—it was very meaningful to have my colleagues stop and set aside a whole chapel to pray for us and for the ministry. At the service, we had pictures of Hilltop before the fire and then pictures of the 57 acres of Hilltop after the fire. There were pictures of Gene walking on the gray, smoke-filled, moonscape path next to the house, and they set the slideshow to Amy Grant's moving song, "After the Fire."

There was not a dry eye in that packed chapel. That service gave me permission to let go of my grief too. I felt very supported by that service.

Also, as the fall began to turn into winter, a practical matter reared its ugly head: because of the fire, erosion had become a real worry up on the mountainside. Because so many of the trees were gone or damaged, there weren't strong root systems holding the soil in place anymore. So the worry was that when the rains started coming, and then the snow, there could be damaging mudslides.

So we let people know that we were going to have to spread hay all over the property—there were 57 acres of it, remember, in order to mitigate the damage that could be caused by the mud and the rains.

A bunch of Talbot students volunteered to come up to help—and even my dean, Dennis Dirks, and his wife, Karen, came up and used their pitchforks with the best of them!

Gene

I had a friend, Phil Mandeville, who loaded a whole semi-truck up with hay and drove it up there. We couldn't get the semi all the way up to the property—the roads got too curvy and narrow for it—and so we had to drive pickup trucks down to the semi, load their beds up with hay there, and then drive them back up to Hilltop.

JUDY

That was the beginning of our clean-up efforts, and I'm glad we had something so obvious to work on, because every other next step just felt…so elusive. It was hard to get started with those "next steps" I'd so calmly talked to the news crew about. It wasn't just hard on a practical level either. It was hard on an emotional level.

Every time we'd go up to the property to do some sort of work, it felt like this heavy fog settled over my shoulders—it was like an unwanted, invisible shawl that I just could not pull off.

You see, the beauty up there was gone. Where once you went up to Hilltop and were immediately drawn into the presence of God by the beauty all around you, now you went up and just wanted to weep.

I went up there and I thought, *How can this place once again become a refuge that brings people peace and healing? How can there be joy again in the midst of such devastation?*

I didn't see how it was possible.

GENE

Restoring Hilltop's beauty was a step I couldn't see either. But there was one next step that was crystal-clear: dealing with the insurance claim for the fire and, Lord willing, using the resulting money to finally retire Hilltop's mortgage.

I took on that step, with help from the Board. One of our board members insisted we hire an outside resource, a company that had helped him settle a past claim. There can be a lot of paperwork and legalese when it comes to claims this large, but I didn't agree that it was necessary, especially because this company was going to take 10% of any resultant payout as compensation for their work. So, in our case, the payout was looking to be about $850,000 to the ministry, and then this company, if they negotiated that claim on our behalf, was going to walk away with $85,000.

So I asked the company rep, "Well, the house is clearly a total loss, so what makes you think the insurance won't pay out the full amount?"

He said, "Well, they just don't."

I said, "Yes, but what if they do?"

He said, "Well, we'll step away."

And I thought, *Oh really?* So I worked on the paperwork, and had a clause to that effect put in.

As it turned out, the insurance companies were dealing with so many claims from the disaster that they just wanted to settle anything they could. The fact that we had this company there representing us too...I don't know. It might have made a difference, it might not have. But the insurance people wrote us a check for the full $850,000, and I paid the company helping us out for their time and effort, but not nearly the huge 10% they'd originally been wanting.

I think that ended up being another instance of the Lord going before us: we were able to preserve more of the ministry's resources—resources that, it turned out, we would need later.

But some of those resources we used right away, and for a very good reason: we were finally able to retire the mortgage. In December of 2003, right before Christmas, I sent a payoff on the loan to the lender who'd originally helped us buy the property—the fellow that took on investments that the big banks wouldn't take. I thanked him for his faith in us, and it felt good to know that we'd been able to repay that faith, in full.

It was a really strange way to get there—paying off the property with insurance money because we'd sustained a total loss—but Hilltop, as a ministry, was finally debt-free.

Just like it had been in Judy's original vision.

Judy

More work on the property followed, bit by bit—and, as always, we found that others came alongside to help us.

Gene

At first, it was our neighbors, the other victims of the fire. We all had timber on our property now that was salvageable—redwood and cedar trees that were dead, that weren't going to grow anymore, but that could be harvested for lumber. Their outsides were charred, but there was still good, usable wood at their hearts.

So all of the neighbors banded together and hired a forester to come in and take the timber. We ended up getting a nice chunk of change for all of that lumber. It was a really odd way to get an influx of cash, but we were grateful for it—though the foresters left a huge mess when they were done. There was this huge woodpile, all of the scraps, that was the height of a two- or three-story house!

I looked at that mess and thought, *What have we done?*

JUDY

But eventually we got help with that too. Gene partnered with our neighbors again, and we all applied for a government grant to help replant trees on all these burned-out acres.

GENE

Originally, the grant was meant to address the bark beetle problem that had been plaguing the California forests, and then that grant somehow got attached to the work to repair the fire damage.

I guess, fire or beetles, the government didn't want to see the forest destroyed!

The people administering the grant decided that they wanted to make Hilltop the poster child for fire abatement.

And so they planted trees.

JUDY

Thousands of trees! I think there were 30,000-40,000—they had a quota of so many per acre. Soon, the property was full of thousands of tiny, bright green seedlings, lifting their minuscule branches up to heaven.

Gene

The state, through that grant, also cleared up the land, which was a real blessing, and the grant included some money for the property owners, too.

It was fascinating watching them do the work of planting the trees. They planted each seedling along with this little tiny bit of moisture. They said that probably 60% of the seedlings they planted would survive, and they did! Today you can go up there and see all of these pine trees—they're about ten feet tall at this point.

Judy

It does look better now, with the trees beginning to gain height. But it's still not what it was, and in that year or two after the fire, even the tiny seedlings weren't enough to restore the beauty that had been there before the fire. I mean, the seedlings were so tiny you could hold one in your hand. They didn't have a huge effect on the big picture you saw when you stood on the property. It was still like a moonscape up there, razed and desolate.

The little saplings held out hope that someday—decades from now—the property might regain its former beauty. But as it stood, it was still a barren land...and the house was still gone. Pastors could not come up on retreat here—there was nowhere for them to retreat *to.*

And I wasn't sure if there would be, ever again.

After that, we entered into another time of waiting.

GENE

We knew the ministry was going to go on. We had the full intention of rebuilding on the property and starting over.

But we had to take some time to figure out how.

JUDY

The first summer after the fire, we got out our little tent that we had used years before, and we went camping. That first year, we were just kind of catching our breath.

Then, in the second year, we went camping again. That year, while on that vacation, I found myself praying, *Lord, we just have to restart this ministry somehow. Maybe there's another property we could use in the meantime? Something. We just need to do* something.

We thought there wasn't going to *be* a ministry anymore if we didn't do something soon—if we didn't get some kind of interim ministry going.

GENE

In some ways, I was busier than ever with the ministry even though the ministry wasn't *doing* anything at the moment. Managing the grants and the logging of the timber and the insurance...that took a lot of time.

Then an architect came alongside us and helped us create some new plans for rebuilding on that property.

JUDY

We were just about ready to start pulling building permits and to begin anew, but every time I went up to the property, that depression would set in again—that cloud of sadness and grief that settled down upon my shoulders like a heavy shawl that I couldn't take off. The beauty just wasn't there. The call to God wasn't there. The view was still there in some ways, but not that amazing feeling that seemed to call you right into the presence of the Lord.

It was hard for me, but I just couldn't bring myself to pull the building permits, even though so much had been done to restore the property.

What would we do next?

We didn't know.

Gene walking through burned property

Hilltop devastated

Chapter Sixteen

Beginning Again

Judy

For two years after the fire, nothing seemed to change. Gene and I were still busy with the surprising amount of work that comes with managing a property devastated by a natural disaster, but there didn't seem to be much forward progress on actually getting the ministry up and running at full speed again.

The closest we came was with the plans from the new architect who came alongside us. A Chinese firm kindly volunteered some of their time and expertise to help us dream about what we could build on the property—about how we could house the ministry in a new building up there where the previous one had burnt down. They liked the ministry and really wanted to be involved in building the next retreat house, which was so kind of them. We met with them, we talked with them, and we dreamed with them. We went to their place and discussed what we would like to have in a new building—things like how many rooms we would like it to have. We'd run Hilltop long enough now that we had the experience to know what kind of facilities would really be ideal for that kind of ministry. And so they drew up some initial plans.

Gene

They made it easy to have big dreams about what the next retreat house would look like! To be honest, what we came up with was pretty intense: we had this idea for a rather grandiose building, very large and with a courtyard in the center—in some ways, sort of like the structure you see in California's historic missions.

Judy

I think consulting with that architectural firm was important, if only because it got us moving again. It made one thing very clear: we needed to move on. We needed to rebuild.

For a while, that was as far as my thinking got—it was just that one clear thought: *We need to move on; we need to rebuild.* I think I got stuck there for a while, and didn't think more deeply about it. Sometimes the realization of *where I am is not okay* is so ground-shaking that it takes you a while to move on to the questions that should logically come next. Questions like, *Okay, if I have to move on, what should that look like? Where should I move on* to? *Where should I* not *go? Which important principles should guide my next steps?*

Realizing that we needed to move on, that we needed to rebuild, was a really important step. But it wasn't the end of the journey—it wasn't even actually moving on! That realization was just an impetus towards the next thing, and not the thing itself.

Nevertheless, I felt excited when I looked at those new plans for rebuilding and growth. But then I traveled up to the mountaintop with Gene and...

And it was still a desolate wasteland. Unbeautiful. Uninspiring.

I couldn't bring myself to move forward there.

Gene

So we did not engage the architects for rebuilding—it just didn't seem like the right option.

We went on with life. I kept managing the upkeep of the property as it was and Judy continued teaching at Biola University.

For two years, nothing seemed to change.

Until something did.

Judy

I mentioned that we spent two of our summer vacations in a small tent camping. After all, we didn't have our trailer anymore—it had burned in the fire! But tents still let you get out into those beautiful parts of nature that soothe the soul. Despite the loss of the trailer, which was our favorite way to camp, we were still grateful our work allowed us to take those weeks off, and that we had the resources to travel to national parks and the like. We don't—and didn't—take that for granted.

As I said, that first summer, we were just catching our breaths.

But during the second summer, I found myself growing restless. I found that I had accepted what had happened to Hilltop. As awful as it was, I had accepted it. I had grieved it.

I wanted to move on.

So what did I do? Well, I began to pray—I began to pray *earnestly.*

That second summer, we were camping up in one of our favorite places in the world: Banff, a gorgeous region of Alberta. Located in the Canadian Rocky Mountains, Banff is famous for its amazing alpine scenery: high, majestic mountains, sprawling green meadows, and stunning, blue, crystal-clear lakes.

There, on our summer vacation, in that beautiful place, I began to earnestly seek the Lord's will regarding what we should do next.

GENE

As we talked about what we should do next, we had practical considerations in our minds as well as spiritual ones. The practical conversation Judy and I were having went something like this: *Well, we were just about to pull permits for these new architectural plans, but the truth is that rebuilding, if we go ahead with it, will take years. Can the ministry afford to take years—even* more *years—to get up and running again? If it takes so much time to rebuild, isn't it possible that we'll lose the ministry altogether in the meantime? Maybe what we need is an interim ministry. Maybe...*

That was what the practical discussion looked like. But that logistical conversation was running alongside a more intangible feeling of discontent, of confusion, of pondering... just a feeling that something was *wrong*. That we hadn't found the right answer yet.

JUDY

So we took all of that to God in our prayers.

In some ways, what we were doing fits in with what I'd spent years teaching our students about at the Institute for Spiritual Formation (ISF) at Biola. One of our main topics at ISF is Soul Care—which is fundamentally nurturing the relational, cognitive, emotional, moral, and physical parts of the soul. This takes trust: both in God, and in His people who He sends to help you. You have to be willing to be *vulnerable* for soul care to work. You have to open up your heart to the Holy Spirit's work.

You can see this kind of vulnerability in David, when he writes:

Search me, God, and know my heart;
test me and know my anxious thoughts.
See if there is any offensive way in me,
and lead me in the way everlasting. (Ps. 139)

In that psalm, David holds himself open before God—he doesn't try to hide his fears or worries. He welcomes God's judgment because he trusts it will also come with God's direction, with God's provision.

Soul care is deconstructive—at least, it is in the beginning. It takes you into your weaknesses. It shows you the truth about yourself in your weaknesses, and then shows you that God still loves you *there.* He loves you as much in your weaknesses as He does in your strengths.

It's presenting ourselves to God—as we actually are, in truth—that allows us to be changed. We have to offer ourselves first. We give up our own lives to God, so that Christ's life can be revealed in us (see 2 Cor. 4:11).

And this isn't a "one and done" sort of a thing! We're human, mortal, fallible, and forgettable. Our emotions shift not just day to day or hour to hour, but minute to minute—sometimes even second to second! Since we're so changeable, we have to *continually* make a practice of offering ourselves to God, of seeking His face.

When we have students—many of them pastors-to-be—at ISF learning soul care, we try to point them towards the model that Jesus Himself provides. You can see an example of how Jesus practiced soul care in John 21, when He speaks to Peter. Peter, of course, had just recently denied even knowing Jesus when Jesus was on trial for His life. The scriptures record that Peter wept bitterly once he realized what he'd done—but it was too late; he'd done it. He'd turned his back on his Lord.

How could he be restored? How could he be forgiven? And, even once he *was* forgiven, how could he believe in that forgiveness?

If you look at what Jesus does with Peter as recorded in that chapter, it's so kind, so tender. And yet so full of unflinching truth. He knows what Peter did. He knows Peter inside and out. And so He asks Peter, basically, to tell the truth about himself. He gently leads Peter into a confession of Peter's own love for Him—but in a way that makes it clear that He knows Peter failed, and yet He doesn't see that as the end. There's more work for Peter to do. There's more love for Peter to grow into.

Discipleship isn't a one-time thing. It continues throughout the disciple's life, as he or she continues to follow Jesus.

And so all of that—all of that knowledge I'd led our students through—all of that was something I experienced in a new and revelatory way myself as I prayed during that camping trip that summer. We'd gone through the fire, and we were battered and bruised, and the future was unclear, and yet I knew it wasn't the end. I knew there was more soul care to be done—both by Jesus towards us, and by us towards those He'd called us to minister to.

So I began to earnestly practice what I taught others: I began to diligently seek the Lord's will. I tried to tell the truth about myself as I prayed. I tried to tell the truth about the ministry, as best as I could, to God. I wanted to present myself to Him honestly. I wanted to present myself honestly and to be transformed.

And I was honest about one other desire.

I was honest that I wanted the ministry transformed too.

And not just transformed.

Reborn.

Gene

When we came back from that camping trip to Banff, we hadn't received any money for the ministry in a good year and a half. The first six months after the fire, we'd received some donations. And we had some money in the bank, of course, and there was the insurance money and the lumber money that we intended to put into the new building. But there hadn't been any real financial movement from donors for about eighteen months.

So that's where we were at the end of that summer. We were praying the Lord would show us how to restart the ministry, and, to be honest, we were a bit fixated on the idea of finding some kind of an interim property we could use—perhaps something we could rent—just so that we could start holding retreats again. We were hoping for an interim plan that would keep us from losing the ministry entirely during the long time we expected it would take to build something new.

So: no retreats for about two years now. No donations for about a year and a half.

By all external signs, the ministry of Hilltop was dead.

But God was not done with it yet.

Not by a long shot.

Judy

We came back home and the school year started up again. One day, I went to school. All of us on the faculty have little mailboxes by our doors, so on my way in, I stopped to check my box.

There, to my surprise, I found…a check! A check for a thousand dollars! It was made out to the ministry at Hilltop.

What's more, I knew the person who gave it and, from my perspective, they didn't *have* a thousand dollars to give. I wondered if the Lord had done some miraculous work of provision in their life, and if this donation represented a gift of thanksgiving from them—if it was their way of passing on the miracle.

So, I was surprised, but…it wasn't *that* astonishing. Unexpected, but not…not *that* odd.

I went through my day, taught my classes, and came home.

And, of course, just like I had at school, I checked my mailbox at home.

There I found…another check. Made out to the ministry at Hilltop.

This time, it was for *$5000.*

Well.

That…that wasn't just unexpected. That looked more like a coincidence.

And as we've noted before: coincidences usually aren't actually coincidences.

They're more often a sign that Someone—Someone who can orchestrate *every* circumstance in our lives—is calling us to pay attention.

I looked at the check, the second one in a day, eighteen months since we'd seen any donation to the ministry at all, and I thought, *God is doing something here.*

But I still didn't know *what* He was doing.

Gene

We'd been through enough since Judy's original vision to know that a "coincidence" like this meant that we needed to be keeping our eyes wide open, looking for signs of what God had next for us.

Judy and I talked about it, and we just kept coming back to the fact that we needed to practice awareness. We needed to be alert and watch for what God was going to do.

What ended up coming next was a call from our daughter's father-in-law, who shared a real estate business with our daughter's husband, Jerry.

"I'm up in Idyllwild," he said, "and I saw some properties. I think you might be able to do something up here."

Well, that felt like a call to action for sure! So I agreed to go up and meet him up in Idyllwild, with Judy planning to follow a few days later, after she'd finished her teaching responsibilities for the week. We'd been looking and listening for the Lord's prompting, and so we were open to Jerry's dad's suggestion when it came.

Judy

Idyllwild was, like Arrowhead, in the mountains near Los Angeles, but rather than being in the San Bernardino mountains to the north, like our burned-out property was, Idyllwild was a small community in the San Jacinto mountain range, which was more directly east of the city.

The topography around Idyllwild is similar to that in the Arrowhead area—the San Jacinto mountains are also made of granite, and are covered with pines, firs, cedars, and oaks. Like the San Bernardino range, the San Jacintos also catch the storms coming off of the ocean and wring out the rain from them before the weather systems can pass on, their moisture spent, to sweep over the deserts to the east.

GENE

I'd spent the few days before Judy came up looking over several possible properties with Jerry's dad, Don Jervis. By the time Don and I returned to the city, I had our itinerary scoped out. Judy and I went up and I took Judy along to the places that looked like possibilities, driving down the narrow mountain roads to one property after another.

JUDY

I was so grateful to Gene and to Jerry's dad for the legwork they'd done ahead of time, and that only made it worse when I looked around the possibilities and realized, *This isn't it.*

I didn't want that to be my reaction! But I couldn't help it. *This isn't the same,* I thought, as I looked around. The areas I saw just didn't have the same call to prayer that I'd felt with the beauty of the original Hilltop property. They didn't feel like places of retreat and rest.

I thought, *I don't think this is quite what God wants us to have.*

But I felt terrible for thinking that.

Gene

After a morning of touring around the various possibilities, we were feeling discouraged. It was hard to think we'd spent all this time up on this mountain just to run into another dead end.

We decided, though, to go ahead and have lunch up there in Idyllwild before heading back down. Might as well be good citizens and put a few dollars into the local economy, right? That's important in places that rely on tourism, and almost all of the small mountain towns up around Los Angeles do.

Judy

It was a beautiful October day and still warm enough to eat outside, so we were attracted to this restaurant called "Gastronome." It was an unusual name, but it was such a quaint little place. It was on the edge of the town and had a tree-covered patio. The outdoor tables had green umbrellas, white tablecloths, and green napkins. It was the kind of place that just called out to you to sit and be refreshed as your body was nourished with incredibly good food. So we settled down to have lunch, letting our eyes feast on the beauty around us there in Idyllwild. From our vantage point on the restaurant's patio, we could see Lilly Rock, a peak that many hikers and climbers travelled to Idyllwild to enjoy.

While we sat there, waiting for our order, we felt rather depressed and sorry for ourselves, despite the lovely setting. There might have even been a few tears, because God still wasn't showing us what we wanted to see—which was a way for the ministry to start up again. But then I spotted something out of the corner of my eye—something seemingly small, seemingly insignificant.

But it turned out that what I saw changed everything.

Chapter Seventeen

A New Home for Hilltop

Judy

There we were, sitting at the restaurant, waiting for our order. We were a bit grumpy and disappointed and hungry—nothing terrible, but it certainly hadn't felt like a banner day.

Then, out of the corner of my eye, I spotted something on the table: a real estate magazine. *Huh*, I thought. *I guess the theme of the day is "houses for sale."*

Well, there was nothing else to do, so I started paging through it.

It was a local magazine, specific to the area, so I flipped past listing after listing of snug little mountain cottages, palatial mountain getaways, and ordinary mountain cabins. *Mountain* this and *mountain* that.

Then I stopped. One particular listing, on one particular page, caught my eye. The listing was titled, "A Private

Shangri-La." *Shangri-La*, of course, was a reference to a legendary hidden paradise—a place of rest and peace.

It was a house with just three bedrooms, plus a small apartment downstairs—small compared to the old house at Hilltop. But something about it struck me. Something about it touched my heart. It felt like God was trying to get my attention.

So, I stuck my finger on the page, looked up, and asked, "Did Jerry call on this one?"

"Yes," Gene said, "But it was sold."

Sold? That didn't seem to fit. Maybe God wasn't trying to get my attention after all. Still… "I think I'd like to see it," I said. "Let's go down to the realtor's office and see if they'll take us over to it."

Gene

We finished our lunch and then I drove us over to the office of the real estate agent listed in the magazine.

Once we'd arrived and told them what we wanted, I asked, "Would you take us to see this property? And, is it really sold?"

"Well…" they hedged.

The real answer was "not quite." What they told us at the office was that they'd received a second offer from a very interested buyer, and that's the point in any sale process when they usually say, "It's sold"—presumably because they feel comfortable that they'll close on this second offer.

They were currently working on the second offer—they were happy with it and the owners were cooperating with the potential buyers to make a deal that everyone could agree to.

But, given that nothing is ever final in real estate until the day that escrow closes, the agent was willing to take us up to the property to look around.

And so that's what we did.

Judy

I walked onto that property and I instantly felt that same thing that I felt at the first Hilltop. This new place had the same beauty, the same call to prayer.

I knew right away that this was where we were supposed to start up the ministry again.

Gene

We both loved the property and decided it was time to get Jerry involved.

The real estate agent had made it clear that the owners were still negotiating with the potential buyers, and so I knew there was still space to make a deal. It wasn't sold—not quite, not yet.

Judy

I told Gene, "Let's call Jerry and see if we can make an offer that's slightly higher than the current offer on the table."

The wonderful thing was that, because of the insurance payout from the fire, we were able to make the owners of this new place a cash offer.

Gene

There was no negotiation needed, like they needed to be doing with their other offer. Our offer was just, "Here's the money you're asking for, all cash, all ready to go."

The owners accepted it and, once more, the ministry of Hilltop had a home.

Judy

When we heard that our offer was accepted, I suddenly remembered something. I remembered Jim Hamel, the man whose name God gave me on the first night of my vision—the man who then later gave the ministry that first large donation: the $10,000 check.

When we had spoken all those years ago, I'd asked him if he believed that God gave people visions. He not only said that he believed God gave visions, but he offered to share his own vision with me. He told me about a dream God had given him, where he'd been in a house filled with fireplaces, and out of those fireplaces flew this steady stream of money. God told him it was money he was going to have and that he was to use it to help others.

God indeed helped him become a wealthy man and he, in turn, was faithful in being generous with his money, helping many, many people, including all of us at Hilltop.

I think that vision he shared with me ended up foretelling what was going to happen to the vision for Hilltop: the money for Hilltop's eventual form *did* come out of a great fire—flying out of the fireplace, as it were.

We had lost everything, but out of that devastating fire, God brought even more beauty.

Because, as it would turn out, Hilltop's new home—even though it started out as a small, three-bedroom house, with a smaller apartment downstairs—would turn out to be a larger, more expansive ministry than ever before.

The day we bought the new house in Idyllwild on behalf of the ministry was the beginning of God bringing beauty out of the ashes.

Out of the true, literal ashes.

God's work is incredible. He indeed can and will do more than we could ever ask or imagine.

Gene

So it was that day in October of 2005—two years after the devastating fire—Hilltop found a new place to call home. That fall and early winter were spent once more preparing a refuge for those who would come up on retreat, and by January, the ministry was in full swing again.

Judy

There was one more significant miracle that happened in the purchase of the house, and the story would be incomplete without sharing it.

The weekend after we purchased the house, the Talbot faculty was on retreat at the nearby Tahquitz Pines Conference Center—also in Idyllwild. During their afternoon break, they joined Gene and me at the new property, to see what God had provided for restarting the ministry and to pray over the new house.

Gene called the man who was selling the house and made an appointment with him regarding buying some of the furnishings of the house as part of the sale. Gene also wanted to give him a brochure to introduce him to the ministry of Hilltop.

The seller was an elderly man of the Jewish faith and a retired research professor from USC, and he was married to a Colombian woman who did not speak much English. God opened his heart to us when he saw the psalms written in our brochure.

He welcomed the Talbot faculty coming to see the house, and they enjoyed talking with him. Talbot's professor of Old Testament, who was fluent in Spanish, spoke with the seller's wife, and it was a blessed conversation.

Before we all left, the faculty stood on the property and prayed that the seller would be gracious with the furnishings in the home. Gene then stayed to negotiate with the owner… and just an hour or two later, he drove to Tahquitz Pines with the news that the owner was giving the house to us as it was—and not removing anything!

This turned out to be such a blessing because we had so much work to do there, and we needed places for our helpers to sleep! We needed places to sit, we needed light for the work. Having all the furnishings remain in place meant there were beds and chairs and lamps for us all.

When we did eventually purchase new furnishings for the house, the extra, older items that were left behind were divided among the Talbot students who had done all the work. God used the owner's generosity to bless everyone!

Gene

Meanwhile, there was a lot of work to do on the new property. We refurbished the entire place. We started redecorating it again—knowing from our past experience at the old Hilltop what kinds of decorations and paint jobs and various other small details make for a restful refuge for ministers, missionaries, and seminarians in need of rest.

Judy

I think Gene's corporate experience did us a lot of good there—both at the old Hilltop and at the new one. He was the one who would direct us towards lots of seemingly small details that ended up adding a great deal to the comfort of the retreat center. He'd recommend things like pillow-top mattress and extra-long beds, so that no one would get a bad night's sleep. Considerate, thoughtful things that ended up making a big difference in the overall experience of the missionaries, ministers, and students who came up at retreat, and a lot of those details were things that came out of his experience of years and years of business travel. He'd stayed overnight at so many different hotels and locations that he knew what a traveler needed in order to find rest in an unfamiliar place—even if that unfamiliar place was set on the side of a beautiful mountain.

Gene

Some of the bigger changes we made were important too—especially adding more bedrooms. We refurbished the basement into a bedroom, for instance.

But even then, with all the work we were putting in and all the changes we were making, we still were thinking of this property as an *interim* property. It was so small; we didn't think it could be Hilltop's new *permanent* home.

Judy

We had some students from the Institute for Spiritual Formation at Biola come up and help us turn some of the lower-floor workrooms into bedrooms. They came up during a conference week at school. Since classes were canceled in order to make room for the conference, they had extra flexibility in their schedules. We had about a dozen of them up there with us that week.

Each of them claimed a room to paint—bless them! Those with carpentry skills turned a researcher's laboratory into a bedroom and converted the cupboards from the lab into closets. They made bedrooms out of the basement's work and storage rooms. God gave us student helpers who had all the building skills and tools we needed at the time—and later on, I watched those same students become gifted spiritual directors! And our friend Leah Hutchinson came up to help us decorate. She picked colors to paint the rooms and carpet samples for the floors, and later went to pick out the new furnishings we needed. We all just worked like a happily buzzing hive of busy bees, moving here and there, working constantly, putting it all together again.

It was so good to be up there with a group of people, working on the ministry! It was like old times, and the camaraderie really warmed my heart.

GENE

Then, in the midst of all our work, came a knock on the door! It was a local realtor, with a surprising message.

He said, "Do you know that the six acres next door to you are up for sale?" I thought for sure that you would be interested in them."

The realtor was a Christian and had heard that what we wanted to create and what we needed was solitude, quiet, and peace. When these six acres came up for sale, he worried about someone buying it and building a home right next door—he worried about our solitude being destroyed.

JUDY

It was a blessing to have him think of us, and we did want to protect Hilltop in any way we could, but…Did *we want to buy those six acres and be totally out of money?* It was such a dilemma!

On the one hand, *Yes*, we wanted to buy it, of course we did! But…we were finally close to operating the ministry the way the Lord had first indicated that we should: debt-free. That had been a clear part of the original vision, and it had taken us so long to get this near to walking in accordance with that instruction. How could we fall away from that now?

But, on the other hand...wouldn't it be a mistake to let the six acres next door sell to someone else? What if our new neighbors were noisy and rowdy? What if the peace and solitude of this new retreat house—a peace and solitude that new retreatants were only now beginning to enjoy—was snatched away again, never to return?

The future was unclear.

Gene

The realtor gave us some more information about the property. He let us know that it had recently dropped out of escrow, which was why it was up for grabs again. "I just think that you're supposed to have this property," he said.

Of course, we didn't have the money to buy the property next door! We'd spent the insurance money on this new house we were—even at that very moment!—fixing up and repairing. We were thinking of the property we were working on now as an interim property, but seeing these new six acres up for sale made us reconsider. Should we sell the old property and buy these six acres? But the old property wasn't even listed for sale yet, and we hadn't even had anyone asking when we *would* put it up for sale.

Which is hardly surprising. I mean, who wants to buy 57 acres of burnt-out land?

Judy

I didn't want to go into debt anymore. Not again. The truth is that being in debt on the old property had kept us from being completely true to the vision God had given us. After all, there had been times, at the old Hilltop, when we'd let people stay at the retreat house who weren't *really* up there to spend time with God. We had to—we had a mortgage, and the ministry needed the money! So if there were no ministers or missionaries or seminary students who were scheduled for a retreat on any particular weekend, we'd let civic groups or the like rent it out.

I knew that the original vision said that we were supposed to be debt-free. This new chance at expanding the ministry's property held out the same temptation to go back into debt. And it *was* tempting. Protecting the peace and solitude of the new retreat house was so important to me. I couldn't bear to sacrifice that.

But I couldn't bear to walk backwards either. I didn't want to step back from the original vision. I wanted us to be faithful—especially since God had already brought us so far and had proved His own faithfulness to us time after time after time.

What was it that we should do? Should we buy it and protect the solitude?

Or should we let it go, and just pray that our new neighbors wouldn't disturb our newfound peace?

It was a very hard decision to make.

Chapter Eighteen

The House of Solitude and the House of Community

Judy

In the aftermath of the fire, Gene and I had had lots of time to reflect on our first years of ministry at Hilltop. When we'd bought the property at Arrowhead, it had seemed so perfect, and we had been so eager to get started in the work God had given us to do, that we'd just gone ahead with it—rushing in with joy.

But in the years that had followed, we'd grown. We'd spent time in the same sort of practices of prayer and solitude in which we'd led all of these pastors and missionaries and seminarians.

I found that I was a different person now than I'd been all of those years ago, and so I was approaching the question of buying these six adjoining acres in a different mindset than I'd had when we were younger.

Over the years, God had helped me learn how to speak what He wanted me to speak, and to follow without doubting.

Gene was a different person now too: he had learned to let go of the corporate career that had been his identity, and had learned how to follow God in faith, fearlessly.

There was a lot of growth that had to happen in me before I could really understand how God wanted us to live and how He wanted us to step forward in faith when He spoke—even though we tried so hard, from the beginning, to obey.

One incident that really cemented this lesson in my mind happened when Gene and I took a trip through Spain with a friend. It was a great trip; we visited a bunch of different old monasteries and studied the roots of Christianity in the country.

One night, after driving too long and too late, we were close to Valencia, and we began to discuss whether we should go down to the beach or drive on to Valencia proper. And I clearly heard God say, *Go to the beach.* But I didn't tell my companions. What I said instead was, "I'd kind of like to go to the beach."

Well, we ended up in Valencia and our things were stolen from our car that night. Actually, *my* things were stolen. My Bible was taken and my suitcase was taken, because they were in the back seat and everyone else's stuff was in the trunk.

I think that incident was God teaching me a lesson: *When I say something to you, I want you to speak.*

I had two or three more experiences like that later on—times when God would say, "Speak, Judy." And, eventually, I did. I found my voice. Through listening for the Spirit of God's voice and then following in obedience, I have learned how to speak what God says to me.

Gene

Judy also had that truth—that her speech is her gift—reflected back to her by her students. One year, at the Institute for Spiritual Formation at Talbot, the graduating class of students gave each of their professors journals—these were gifts to thank the professors for the years of teaching and care they'd poured into these students' lives.

The journals were filled with little slips of paper on which the students had written what each professor had meant to them. One of Judy's said, "You speak truth like a laser that goes straight to the heart."

I think that's because, over the years, Judy has found her voice. She knows how to speak up for the truth that God shows her.

That became important as we contemplated buying this new property.

Judy

The problem with going into debt again was that debt had compromised the ministry in the past. Being in debt, we both felt, had kept us from being completely true to the vision God had originally given me. Hilltop was designed—and really did operate—as a retreat center for pastors and other Christian ministers. But occasionally, at the first Hilltop, when it wasn't booked for a specifically Christian retreat, we'd let other organizations use the property.

And we did that because we needed the money in order to service the debt.

GENE

The circumstances in those early days didn't allow us the time to spend hours contemplating the vision. We were just surviving.

But that changed when we came to Hilltop II.

We were finally ready to embrace the *entire* vision. This new Hilltop would be exactly what God wanted it to be: dedicated to Christians in ministry, in easy driving distance of Los Angeles, and *without debt.*

JUDY

The first steps of the ministry, back at the beginning, had been true steps of faith. But now that God had grown us more, we could do more. We had so much more focus when we got to the second incarnation of Hilltop. We'd been through a refining process: both the vision itself and our own hearts had been refined.

At the beginning, when I heard "debt-free," it didn't seem like it was possible, and so we didn't try for it. God had to grow our faith—and the series of miracles He led us through certainly did the trick!

Gene

Looking back, I can see that God had a lot He wanted to change in my heart, too. Judy's faith and my faith both grew, but in different times and in different ways. Sometimes it felt like she had the gift of faith and I had the gift of realism!

But I had to learn to allow God to lead me where He wanted me to go, and that took time.

Judy

What Gene always did have was a willing heart. That was a gift from God way back in the beginning, and it was that willing heart that led to everything else. Gene is one in a million—he went along with the vision with a strength and a purpose that most men don't have. And his strong leadership skills were a gift to the ministry from the very beginning. I feel blessed to be a wife who is very, very supported by her husband.

And, honestly, his realism brings balance to me. The Lord has used the push-and-pull of our different personalities to accomplish His purposes, and it's been such a blessing to watch that happen. It's been clear from the start that the Lord wanted *both* of us to work together to bring the vision into reality.

So, despite our uncertainty when the neighboring plot of land came up for sale, we took our next steps with hearts full of gratitude.

Gene

With the work crew of students that was already up on the mountain with us, we took time to pray and seek the Lord's will for Hilltop.

At the new property, there was a huge granite boulder embedded in the soil with a view of the valley below and Lilly Rock rising up from the earth, Tahquitz Peak protecting the whole scene. So we took our whole crew out on that rock and we prayed.

Judy

You can see how much we'd learned and grown. We knew right away that, when faced with a big decision, seeking the Lord in prayer was the most important and best thing that we could do!

So we prayed, all of us together. We just spent time asking the Lord to give us guidance, asking Him, *What are we supposed to do here?*

And then the most amazing thing happened—it's incredible the way God will speak to us! We opened our eyes after praying and looked out across the dip in the land to the opposite slope. Out in the distance, on that slope, was another boulder—a giant granite rock formation, shining in bright contrast to the dark, dusky green of the surrounding trees.

The rock looked exactly like a woman kneeling in prayer, with Jesus standing behind the woman.

We all saw it—each one of us thought that was what it looked like. And as we looked, we said, *This is a place of prayer, this is Hilltop permanent! This is not just an interim ministry.*

It was clear that what we were supposed to do was to pray that God would send a buyer for the old, burned-out property back by Arrowhead, so that we could pay for the land adjacent to the new Hilltop without taking on any new debt. It was time to expand the retreat center here in Idyllwild.

So we climbed down from our prayer rock—which we now call Inspiration Point—and said yes to the realtor. We told him that we wanted to buy the adjacent property, in faith that God would send a buyer for the old property.

Gene

That was the other thing: figuring out exactly how to handle the old Hilltop property. Even though we'd gotten the insurance pay-out for the damage—the lost house, etc.—the ministry still owned the actual land and the care of the land was still an ongoing responsibility for me, Judy, and the rest of the board.

It still felt like a desolate moonscape every time we visited it, and it was just so depressing. I remember talking to the board about it.

Sam Metcalf, one of our board members, was the one who eventually gave us just the right piece of direction regarding what we should do with the land. Sam said, "Gene, if in your lifetime this property is not going to be beautiful, let's move on."

So that's what we did. I got a hold of Jerry, our son-in-law again, and said. "Let's put the property on the market."

Jerry did as we asked, and those burned-out 57 acres went up for sale.

Judy

Praying for the sale of the old property was a big ask. We knew that. After all, nothing had happened on the old property for a year. I mean, who wants to buy a bunch of land full of charred wood and ashes?

Still, we stepped out in faith in regard to those six adjacent acres, knowing that land would protect the privacy and solitude we were cultivating at Hilltop, and to pay for it, we put the old property up for sale.

Gene

In the end, the old property was on the market for a *year.*

But all of the sudden, we got a call.

We had one looker.

That one looker became one buyer.

And that was all we needed.

Judy

It was amazing—and it was totally a gift of God. We sold the old property for just under a million dollars—hundreds of thousands of dollars more than we'd paid to buy it in the first place, and when we'd bought it, it'd had a whole gigantic beautiful house on it! Now it sold for a lot more money, and without any house on it at all.

With that sale, the ministry was completely debt-free, had a larger parcel of land up in Idyllwild, *and* had money in the bank.

Gene

It's strange to say, but the old Hilltop property is still sitting empty. A year or two ago, we drove up to it, just to see what had happened to it. The road curving up the slope to where the house was is cracked and weathered, unrepaired. And the foundation of the house still sits on the ground, barren. Nothing's been added, nothing changed.

It's like the land is having its Sabbath rest.

Judy

After that time with the student crew who prayed with us on Inspiration Point, we kept working on refurbishing the house up in Idyllwild. Eventually, it had eight bedrooms with 18 beds, and an apartment with a queen-sized bed.

Hilltop was up and running again. Gene's full-time dedication to the ministry kept him as busy as a man could be—busy and flourishing and loving it.

It has been such a joy to be able to work together in our later years on this project that God had for us.

At this point, all of the seminary students at Talbot come up to Hilltop at least twice during their schooling in order to learn how to pray and be in solitude with the Lord. We see them receiving this deeper love of God, and we see the way their future ministries have poured out of that love that God has given them.

It's really the way ministry is meant to be: as God gives these ministers gifts, they give them away. They are blessed and then they turn around and bless others.

It's such a joy to be a part of that process.

Gene

Now we are able to operate Hilltop the way it's meant to be operated.

We have the freedom to do that now.

Judy

We bought those adjacent acres in 2005, but of course we had other neighbors. In the early days up in Idyllwild, Gene went to meet and talk to them. One of the things he'd said to them was, "You know, *if* you ever want to sell, please come and talk to me," because we knew we wanted to preserve the privacy of the retreat center. We didn't want our good neighbors to sell to someone who might be noisy and run all over the land with ATVs that tore everything up—at least, we didn't want that to happen without having the chance to pray and see if the Lord would want us to buy whatever property was for sale. We wanted to be mindful of protecting the privacy and peace up at Hilltop.

Well, in 2013, one of our neighbors came to talk to us—a man who shared the same small road that Hilltop's property is on. He started the conversation a bit hesitantly, saying, "You know, I never thought I would sell…"

Gene

But the upshot was that he *did* want to sell. And he said, "I want to give you the first option to buy."

We really appreciated that, and we took the time to pray about it, and to talk to the Board—we wanted to see what our board members thought and to give them a chance to pray about it too.

We all agreed that buying the property was a good idea, and we had *some* money in the bank. But not enough. So we sent out a letter to our supporters around Easter time, and by June, people had generously given enough that we were able to make the purchase—debt-free, of course.

Judy

The new addition to Hilltop's property had a house on it—a smaller one. It was an additional acre of land, and a house that has two bedrooms, with four beds total. There's also room to eventually add two to three more bedrooms. So now we have two houses at the retreat center. We call the smaller one The House of Solitude and the larger one The House of Community.

The House of Community only had three bedrooms when we first bought it, plus a small apartment downstairs, but we've continued to grow and remodel and refurbish, and now it has nine bedrooms and seven baths. It's amazing—without changing the footprint of the house itself, we've been able to create these small, wonderful, beautiful bedrooms, so that people can have their own space while they're up on retreat. Each of the bedrooms has a door to the outside, so people can easily slip out into the beauty of God's creation as they pray and contemplate and think.

They have all of their creature comforts met, and so they have no excuse to do anything but what they've come up there to do: to spend time in silence and in the presence of the Lord.

Hilltop is a place of peace, of joy, of ministry, and of love. We praise God for what He has done.

Gene

Doing this ministry has enriched our marriage so much. That's not why we do it, of course, but it's been one of the most significant results of doing it.

Back when Judy was still going to school, when we'd take our vacations, she'd read her schoolbooks to me so I wouldn't be bored while I was driving, and that was one way we grew and learned together. But being in ministry together has been so much more of a significant change in our relationship.

In the beginning of our marriage, we lived in separate worlds. We both lived in our work.

Now, we still live in our work, in a way, but our work is so unified now, and so much more focused on our Lord.

That has been an unspeakable blessing.

Judy

As I think back on the story of Hilltop, I think of a multitude of miracles. Miracles inside of me, inside of Gene, and between the two of us. Those are the spiritual miracles.

Then I think of the more tangible miracles: the provision of land, of furnishings—even of the other people whose dedication was so necessary to bringing Hilltop into existence!

I think our culture likes to think that visions are *instant.* You have a vision and then—boom!—it comes into being.

But through Hilltop, I've learned that bringing visions into existence takes time and it takes a heart willing to learn. We had *so* much to learn! We had to learn how to pray, we had to learn how to connect to people we didn't know yet, we needed to learn how to ask God for what He Himself had *told* us to ask for!

We had to learn how to share the story of God in a way that gave Him glory. I hope that's what we've done here. I hope as you read the story of Hilltop, you hear that visions take time, they take energy, they take patience, they take endurance.

But I hope that you also hear that walking in obedience to God brings so much joy because you get to see how He is at work every single day in every one of us!

So little of Hilltop came about because of us, because of our striving. It was all God. Our part was waiting and obedience.

It's been such an honor to watch how God wanted to shape this vision.

God is the ultimate shaper of visions.

Hilltop House of Community

Hilltop House of Solitude

Epilogue

A House of Prayer and a Promise

Judy

The story of how Hilltop came to be—the vision, the miraculous "coincidences" involving people and money and resources, the fire, the rebuilding—is a story I never get tired of telling. God decided to make a place of rest for His people, and we got to be part of it. For the rest of my life, I will be delighted that I got to be a part of that story.

It's a complete narrative—a story we can tell to others and actually say "The End" when we are finished.

In a way, it's done. We were called, by God's grace we obeyed, and God provided what we needed every step of the way.

The End.

Except…

Except, of course, it isn't the end. Nothing in this world

is final and finished and complete—not until the Lord Jesus returns. Life goes on for all of us, and life goes on for Hilltop too, and so we wanted to share a bit about what the continuing ministry of Hilltop is like today, and how the Lord has continued to work there and show mercy to us and all who go up on the mountain to seek His face in prayer.

Gene

Today Hilltop is a place of renewal for God's people. It regularly serves individuals, groups, and couples that are in ministry, allowing them to have time alone with God in His creation.

Hilltop has two homes, with 22 beds, and 17 acres of land, full of trails and places for meditation. We average about 65% occupancy, and Hilltop is booked most weekends with groups and most weekdays with individual retreats. We do no advertising as we're very affordable; we get our retreatants through referral and word of mouth. We sometimes now even have to turn people away due to lack of time or space.

We're restrictive on usage—only people who want to come and intentionally spend time with God are allowed to use the property. We've had to struggle with that a bit, because sometimes people want to come up just for a quick fix—they want a keynote speaker to instantly fix their lives or they want to treat it more as a vacation. We've had to be adamant about the fact that this is a *renewal* center, and you're only renewed by *the Spirit of God* renewing you.

You have to let Him do the work.

Judy

Back when I was working so many hours in counseling centers with pastors, trying to encourage them and minister to the broken places in them, I'd come to the firm conviction that while care offered in the moment of crisis was important, finding a way to prevent the crises from occurring would be even better.

Hilltop is a part of that answer—it has become a place of preventative care, where people learn to be with their Lord in such a way that much spiritual illness is avoided. Learning to find peace in God's presence is vital to our spiritual health.

Peace, solitude, and the practices of spiritual formation are to the soul what good nutrition, rest, and exercise is to the body. Can crises still occur? Of course. But finding and maintaining the practices of good health can prevent so much distress.

Because I still believe that what pastors often need isn't a cure for illness. Instead, they need a vaccine that keeps them from getting sick in the first place.

Gene

And so we continue to work to provide a place where these practices can be learned. At Hilltop, we provide both full-service retreats and self-service retreats, depending on what the people involved want and need.

We also provide guided retreats and spiritual direction when requested.

We have remained debt-free and operate with a conservative budget. We're in the black every year and maintain a small reserve for emergencies.

And we continue to be blessed by those who come alongside us and help. For instance, one year, we had an intern who helped run things. But it was on an as-needed basis, and wasn't a salaried position. Also, for a long time, Judy's sister and her husband, Helen and Wayne DeMann, served on an as-needed basis and we paid them a modest amount. They added special touches to all that they did, whether cooking, serving meals, or maintaining Hilltop, bringing blessing both to us and to the guests they so warmly received.

Judy

When God gave me the vision for a renewal center, He let me know that I wouldn't be going it alone, and how true that's been! I see that in people like my sister Helen and her husband Wayne, in the members of our board, in...oh, *so* many people down the years! So many individuals and Christian ministries have joined us in this quest. Gene and I have been so blessed by all of our fellow believers who have come alongside us and joined us in bringing the vision into reality.

Hilltop has been God's place from the beginning. It isn't ours; it never has been. When people come up, they can see that it's not Judy and Gene's place: it's God's place, and He's provided it *for them*, so that they could spend more quality time with Him.

Gene

And we can see the multiplying effect the ministry is having down through the years. We now have pastors who, having experienced the ministry at Hilltop while they were in seminary, are now bringing it into the churches where they now minister. So we have sort of this second generation of ministry happening. We've had several graduates who bring the members of their own congregations up and basically replicate the experience for others that we first shared with them.

That's been such a blessing to see.

Judy

Over the past decade or so of ministry, we've had our own times when we've needed others to minister to us. In 2009, I was diagnosed with cancer. That was one hard and long journey. And then, in 2019, Gene was diagnosed with cancer, and that's a journey that we're still on.

Through my cancer journey, I clung to Psalm 23 and its description of God as the good shepherd. The Lord really impressed that psalm on my heart throughout that journey; He *showed* me how He kept me in the green pastures and by the still waters, even as I was suffering. He *showed* me how the anointing oil that psalm speaks of are the intercessory prayers of others. He showed me how you can have joy in the midst of suffering.

And now that Gene is walking through a similar valley, that psalm continues to hold us. I said to Gene, *When tempted to go into the dark, know God is holding you in the green pastures and quiet waters. He is with you.*

We've shared that encouragement with so many people at Hilltop, and, both then and now, we have had to cling to it ourselves.

Gene

Cancer is traumatizing. That's the truth of it. We have to acknowledge that truth and still keep taking our next steps forward, trusting the Lord.

Looking back on the history of Hilltop, I can see how He taught us to do that. Step by step, He's always gone before us. He's been faithful. We don't know the future, but we know Him. We know He won't change.

The vision really has been fulfilled. Even after the fire, the promise held fast, the ministry was restored, and the blessing of Hilltop has flowered, providing retreat and solace to so many hundreds and hundreds of God's people.

Judy

But a few more things happened after we finished writing this book—and what happened was so characteristic of God's faithfulness throughout all of Hilltop's existence that we felt we *had* to include it in this epilogue.

As has happened over and over again in this story, the Lord provided both the *places* and the *people.*

Not long after the events chronicled in the last chapter of this book, someone came to me and said, "It is time to complete the vision of having not only a House of Community and a House of Solitude, but also a House of Prayer." Then that same person, who has a generous heart, was moved by the Spirit of God to hand us a check to complete this vision. I shouldn't be surprised, because I have seen, time and again, how good God is. But that is the journey we're on: a continual journey moving deeper and deeper into the goodness of God. So, all the same, I find myself once again amazed by His kindness! It is there, in the midst of that knowledge of His providence, that I want to continually reside. *Goodness and mercy shall follow me all the days of my life.*

So, we got to work on building a House of Prayer up at Hilltop, and that felt like the capstone on the work up there, because a House of Prayer would ground, tangibly, the purpose of the property. *Hilltop is a place of prayer.* That is what this new building says: the focus of this place is prayer. It is a place to turn your mind, and heart, and will towards God.

GENE

And as of 2022, we can say this: the House of Prayer is complete.

It's a small, one-room building, and when you walk into it, you can feel its peace. It's laid out simply, with white walls, and high wooden beams.

When you walk into it, you face tall windows looking out into the beautiful forest. In front of those windows hangs a beautiful blue-and-green stained-glass cross, specially commissioned for Hilltop.

Judy

The House of Prayer is a promise fulfilled.

But it wasn't the greatest need standing in front of us unfulfilled when we looked at the future of Hilltop. That need, of course, was the need for someone to replace Gene and me. Our hope, this whole time, has been that this ministry would outlive us. But how were we going to find the people with the desire, the gifts, and the calling to take on this work in the decades to come?

Gene

Once again, God provided: Lloyd and Cathy Gilbert came into our lives.

Judy

Or rather, we should say, Lloyd and Cathy came *back* into our lives—I had been Lloyd's professor when he'd been going to seminary at Talbot twenty-five years earlier! He got in contact with us again to see if they could use Hilltop for his daughter's wedding. We decided to get together as couples and had lunch up on Hilltop's deck, overlooking the rocks and the trees.

Gene

Lloyd and Cathy shared what they'd been doing since we'd last talked. It turned out that after completing his BA, Lloyd was hired by Rolling Hills Covenant Church, where he pastored for twenty-three years!

But recently he'd begun to feel a call to transition out of youth ministry, and he was in the middle of interview processes with two other churches.

JUDY

We talked about that, and we also talked about our mutual love for Idyllwild—it turned out that they'd grown up in the nearby Banning Pass area, and Lloyd's grandfather actually owned a property up in Idyllwild, so Lloyd had grown up taking family vacations near Hilltop! Now well-seasoned adults with a family of their own, Lloyd and Cathy also owned property up there, and they still loved the Idyllwild area deeply.

At some point in the conversation, Cathy mentioned, "We've always wanted to run a B&B." This rang a bell in my own mind and heart, and I couldn't help but think, *Are these the next people that the Lord wants to run Hilltop?*

GENE

The following weeks brought more meetings, conversations, prayer, consultations, and deep discernment. Lloyd and Cathy prayed long and hard about whether they were supposed to make this transition in their lives—whether they were supposed to be the next caretakers of Hilltop. As Lloyd said, this would be "a deep dive."

JUDY

But it turned out that it was a dive they were supposed to say yes to! After that long period of discernment, Lloyd and

Cathy were offered and accepted the role of caretakers at Hilltop. They are now apprenticing with us. In the beginning, we ran the retreats together and started transitioning much of the cleaning, cooking, and heavier labor to them. But soon they were running the retreats, and doing all of the needed large and small tasks, under our guidance.

As I watch them work so faithfully and well, I feel such a peace in my heart about the years to come here at Hilltop.

Gene

And they came along at exactly the right time: it was in this same season that Judy and I found ourselves needing to begin our own transition. But for us, it was time to transition out. The ministry at Hilltop had become too much for us to handle on our own, but it was clear that the Lord, as always, knew our needs even better than we ourselves did. He was walking before us and making provision for someone else to take on the burden. The timing was incredible. The Lord provided.

Judy

Over the summer of 2021, during the Covid pandemic, the Gilberts built another room onto their cabin in Idyllwild, sold their home in Harbor City (just south of Los Angeles), and moved full-time up to the mountains—even though Lloyd is now taking classes at the Institution of Spiritual Formation at Biola, learning how to be a spiritual director. He drives down to Biola University to attend class, because he wants to be even better prepared for the work at Hilltop. This training will only build on the gifts he already has developed in his many years of being a pastor.

Lloyd and Cathy have as much excitement as I had when I first got the vision. No one but God could have given them that joy in the work, that zest and energy for the vision.

Over and over, God has provided. I give Him glory for the fact that we *never* had to worry about this transition—the Lord provided everything we needed.

He is so faithful.

Gene

The story of Hilltop is the story of a vision—but it is also a story of miracles, of provision, and of faithfulness. God is so good. He gave us a vision of providing a place of rest for His people, and He fulfilled that promise.

We trust that He will continue to fulfill it, as we continue to follow Him, deeper and deeper into His goodness.

May all of our rest be in Him.

The End. *For now.*

Hilltop House of Prayer

Interior of the House of Prayer

ACKNOWLEDGEMENTS

The story of Hilltop Renewal Center reveals that God used many donors, supporters, helpers, encouragers, and others to make His vision a reality. Time and again God brought the right person to the right place at the right time to make sure His will was accomplished. It was always God walking before us preparing the way. He connected people, places and events, and we are so thankful, but it was always Him doing the work and it was no exception with the writing of this book which tells the story.

At one of our Institute for Spiritual Formation faculty meetings which we have twice a month, I shared with my colleagues that Gene and I had always wanted the Hilltop story to be written. Dr. Betsy Barber, my partner in training students in spiritual direction, responded, "My daughter Jessica Snell does this kind of work and she is an excellent writer." That was yet another Holy Spirit moment. What a huge blessing Jessica's rendering of this story has been. Her keen ability to relate Gene and my thoughts, emotions, and experiences, weaving and organizing them into a story that is inviting, truthful, and winsome is truly the work of the Holy Spirit in her. Her writing is truly a gift to us and to those who will read this book. You truly captured the power of the story. Thank you, Jessica, for listening to us relive the story and for listening to the Holy Spirit in how it should be told. We will forever be grateful.

Thank you to Asio Creative and Natalie Lauren Design for the care and expertise you took in helping us publish this book. It has blessed us so much to see this story be written so others can open their eyes to God's faithfulness. Drew and Natalie, you truly enhanced this work with your artistry and expertise. May God bless you for this service to His kingdom.

Gene and I would also like to thank each person named in this book for opening your heart to the Holy Spirit's work and responding generously with your gifts when the Holy Spirit prompted you to support and encourage us. Each one of you assisted in this mighty work of God and we are eternally grateful for your hospitality to His vision and your generous response.

Finally, we would like to thank all those who have found and renewed their home with God at Hilltop Renewal Center, responding to His call to find rest and peace from the busyness of this world. You are a part of this story. May what God has done *in you* be written on invisible pages for us to all read in our eternal home. Our home with God.

About Hilltop

To see pictures of Hilltop both before and after the fire, please visit:
https://www.hilltoprenewal.org/about/.

For information about Hilltop's House of Community, please visit:
https://www.hilltoprenewal.org/community/.

For information about Hilltop's House of Solitude, please visit:
https://www.hilltoprenewal.org/solitude/.

About the Authors

Gene TenElshof

Gene TenElshof is the president of Hilltop Renewal Center, where he is responsible for running the center, booking events, filing government forms, promoting and maintaining the center, and hosting and being hospitable to guests at Hilltop.

Before leaving the corporate world to devote himself to full-time ministry at Hilltop, Gene served in high-ranking positions at several national companies, including serving as Vice President of Sales Lander Company, District Manager at Johnson & Johnson, and Regional Manager at Miles Laboratories (Bayer, Inc.). His responsibilities at these companies involved overseeing tens of millions of dollars of sales, as well as managing brokers, salespeople, and other employees.

Judy TenElshof

Dr. Judy TenElshof is a professor at the Institute for Spiritual Formation at Talbot School of Theology/Biola University and is the Director of Talbot's Spiritual Formation Core. Her goal is to have all Talbot students understand the nature, process, and practices of spiritual growth and to have them experience deeper intimacy with God and others. Her expertise as a teacher, conference speaker, pastoral counselor, and spiritual director is in helping individuals and families grow relationally, morally, and spiritually.

She has established and directed counseling centers in churches and Christian schools and is founder of Hilltop Renewal Center for Christian leaders. She co-edited the book *Women and Men in Ministry*, is the author of several journal articles, and contributed chapters to *Foundations of Ministry: An Introduction to Christian Education for a New Generation*, *Short-Term Missions Boom: The Guide to International and Domestic Involvement*, *The Christian Education Dictionary*, and *Following Jesus Christ: The New Testament Message for Discipleship for Today*.

She has been married to her husband, Gene, for over fifty years, and together they have two children and seven grandchildren.

Made in the USA
Middletown, DE
18 February 2022

61381875R00166